Afghan Favorites

the Needlecraft Shop

A crocheted afghan brings life and love to a room. Crochet is unique among many other needlecrafts in that no machine can reproduce its stitches – the stitches can only be created by hand, lovingly, one by one. The soft and cozy finished product is comforting to everyone from newborn babies to great-grandparents.

This collection of afghans is sure to inspire you with its variety of styles, colors, textures and patterns. Whatever your decorating scheme, you'll find the afghan design you need to complete each room with a generous dollop of color and handmade charm. Each pattern is complete with materials list and easy-to-follow instructions, as well as gorgeous, full-color photographs and diagrams. Everyone will find beautiful designs that are fun to make.

A harvest of afghan patterns in every color and design – what a treat for a crocheter! A masterpiece afghan made with beautiful yarns can become the focal point of a room and at the same time remain handy for cozying up on a long and chilly winter evening.

This cream-of-the-crop collection contains original creations from the world's premier afghan designers. Chosen from the most popular afghans featured in *Crochet Home* and *Hooked on Crochet* magazines, each design is a tested and proven favorite of designers and crocheters alike. Enjoy!

INTRODUCTION

Publisher: Donna Robertson
Editorial Director: Carolyn Brooks Christmas
Design Director: Fran Rohus
Creative Director: Greg Smith
Production Director: Ange Workman

Editorial
Editor: Lorretta Blevins
Associate Editors: Jana Robertson, Trudy Atteberry,
Pauline Rosenberger, Kristine Hart
Proofreader: Mary Lingle
Editorial Assistants: Janice Kellenberger, Jessica Rice
Publisher's Assistant: Marianne Telesca

Photography
Art Directors: Rusty Lingle, Diane Simpson, Dan Kraner
Photographers: Renée Agee,
Tammy Cromer-Campbell, Mary Craft
Pages 2 and 3 Photos: Nancy Sharp
Cover Photo: Mary Craft

Production
Assistant Production Director: Betty Gibbs Radla
Technical Director \ Production: John J. Nosal

Book Design
Art and Production: Dan Kraner
Dan Kraner Design, Berne, IN

Product Design
Design Coordinator: Brenda Wendling

Business
President: Jerry Gentry
Vice President \ Customer Service: Karen Pierce
Vice President \ Marketing: Greg Deily
Vice President \ M.I.S.: John Trotter

Credits
*Sincerest thanks to all the designers, manufacturers and other
professionals whose dedication has made this book possible. Special
thanks to Klaus Rothe of Sullivan Rothe Design, Berne, IN,
Tom Buckley and Susan Price of JTM Colorscan, Ft. Worth, TX, and
Lori Powers of R.R. Donnelly & Sons Co., Chicago, IL.*

Library of Congress Cataloging-in-Publication Data
ISBN: 0-9638031-1-5
First Printing: 1994
Library of Congress Catalog Card Number: 93-86080
Published and Distributed by *The Needlecraft Shop, Inc.*
Printed in the United States of America.

Contents

Autumn Colors

Romantic Lace

Homespun Country

Rich Textures

Classic Ripples

Just for Baby

One-Piece Favorites

Marvelous Motifs

Cozy Quilts

General Instructions

utumn Colors

In all their glory, the rich vermillions,
golds and browns of autumn inspire
the creation of afghans as splendid as
nature's palette. Stitch an afghan
suggested by a stunning bouquet of
sunflowers drying in the late summer
sun, or golden wheat gently rippling in
the breeze in the days before the harvest.

Indian Summer

by designer Eleanor Albano

Interesting wedges form zigzag stripes in warm desert shades of turquoise, peach and brown. Finish with a matching narrow border for understated polish.

Finished Size

57" x 69".

Materials

Fuzzy worsted-weight yarn — 25 oz. brown, 7 oz. each lt. turquoise, turquoise, lt. peach and peach; tapestry needle; J crochet hook or size needed to obtain gauge.

Gauge

4 wedges and 4 sc = 3½"; 4 rows = 3".

Skill Level

★★ Average

Instructions

Afghan

Note: For **wedge**, ch 4, sc in 2nd ch from hook, hdc in next ch, dc in last ch.

Row 1: With brown, ch 182, sc in 2nd ch from hook, (wedge, skip next 2 chs of starting ch, sc in next ch on starting ch) across, turn, fasten off (61 sc, 60 wedges).

Row 2: Join turquoise with sl st in first sc, ch 3, *(sc in top of next wedge; working in opposite side of ch on wedge, sc in next ch, hdc in next ch*, dc in next ch, skip next sc) across to last wedge; repeat between **, dc next ch and last sc tog, turn, fasten off (241 sts).

Row 3: Join lt. turquoise with sc in first st, wedge, skip next 2 sts, sc in next st, (wedge, skip next 3 sts, sc in next st) across leaving last ch-3 unworked, turn, fasten off (60 wedges).

Row 4: With brown, repeat row 2, **do not** fasten off.

Row 5: Ch 1, sc in first st, wedge, skip next 2 sts, sc in next st, (wedge, skip next 3 sts, sc in next st) across leaving last ch-3 unworked, turn, fasten off.

Row 6: With peach, repeat row 2.

Row 7: With lt. peach, repeat row 3.

Rows 8-9: Repeat rows 4 and 5.

Rows 10-76: Repeat rows 2-9 consecutively, ending with row 4.

Row 77: Ch 1, sc in each st across with 3 sc in corner st; (working in ends of rows across first side, sc in each sc and 2 sc in each dc on ends of rows, fasten off); working on opposite side of afghan, join brown with sc in same st as first st, sc in same st; repeat between ( ).∞

Heartland Harvest

by designer Lucia Karge

The wheat-like stitch pattern on this unusual throw brings to mind late-summer fields ready for harvest. Crochet this take-along design in blocks, then connect them all together.

Finished Size

48½" x 60".

Materials

Bulky-weight yarn — 45 oz. tan, 17 oz. turquoise and 10 oz. pink; tapestry needle; H crochet hook or size needed to obtain gauge.

Gauge

3 dc sts = 1"; 2 dc rows = 1½".

Skill Level

★★ Average

Instructions

Square (make 12)

Row 1: With tan, ch 35, dc in 4th ch from hook, dc in each ch across, turn (33).

Note: For **diagonal stitch (diagonal st)** *(see fig. 28, page 158),* skip next st, dc in each of next 3 sts; working over last 3 sts made, insert hook in skipped st, yo, draw up 1"-long lp, yo, draw through both lps on hook.

Rows 2-3: Ch 3, dc in next st, diagonal st across with dc in each of last 3 sts, turn (7 diagonal sts).

Rows 4-5: Ch 3, dc in each st across, turn (33).

Rows 6-16: Repeat rows 2-5 consecutively, ending with row 4, **do not** turn at end of last row.

Rnd 17: Working around outer edge in ends of rows and in sts, ch 2, 2 hdc in same st, *(hdc in next row, 2 hdc in next row) 8 times, 3 hdc in next st, hdc in each st across* with 3 hdc in last st; repeat between **, join with sl st in top of ch-2, **turn,** fasten off (122).

Rnd 18: Join turquoise with sl st in center st of any corner, ch 2, 2 hdc in same st, hdc in each st around with 3 hdc in center st of each corner, join, **turn** (130).

Notes: When changing colors *(see fig. 15, page 156),* work over dropped color. Pick up as needed. Always drop yarn to same side of work.

For **puff stitch (puff st)** *(see fig. 26, page 158),* yo, insert hook in next st, yo, draw up ½"-long lp, (yo, insert hook in same st, yo, draw up ½"-long lp) 5 times, yo, draw through all 10 lps on hook, yo, draw through last 2 lps on hook.

Rnd 19: Sl st in next st, ch 3, 2 dc in same st changing to tan in last st made, dc in each of next 3 sts changing to turquoise in last st made, dc in each of next 3 sts changing to tan in last st made; working in established color pattern, dc in each st around with 3 dc in center st of each corner, join with sl st in top of ch-3, **turn,** fasten off both colors (138).

Rnd 20: Join pink with sl st in center st of any corner, ch 2, 2 hdc in same st, hdc in each st around with puff st in center st of each turquoise group and 3 hdc in each corner, join with sl st in top of ch-2, **turn,** fasten off.

Rnd 21: Repeat rnd 18, fasten off.

Holding right sides together, working through both thicknesses, with pink, sc squares together in three rows of four squares each.

For **edging,** working around outer edge, with tan, repeat rnd 18, fasten off.

Sunflower Bouquet

by designer Katherine Eng

This bright and sunny afghan is a medley of cheerful autumn colors. Each beautiful block features the flower of the sun, and the afghan is edged with a glorious ripple border.

Finished Size

Block is 6" square. Afghan is 43½" x 55½".

Materials

Worsted-weight yarn — 29½ oz. yellow, 12½ oz. each dk. yellow and brown, 8 oz. green; tapestry needle; F crochet hook or size needed to obtain gauge.

Gauge

4 dc sts = 1"; 2 dc rnds = 1½".

Skill Level

★★ Average

Instructions

Block (make 48)

Rnd 1: With brown, ch 4, sl st in first ch to form ring, ch 1, 8 sc in ring, join with sl st in first sc (8 sc).

Rnd 2: Ch 1, 2 sc in each st around, join, fasten off (16).

Rnd 3: Join yellow with sc in first st, 3 dc in next st, (sc in next st, 3 dc in next st) around, join, fasten off (24 dc, 8 sc).

Note: For **shell**, 5 dc in next st.

Rnd 4: Join dk. yellow with sc in 2nd dc of any 3-dc group, skip next dc, shell in next sc, skip next dc, (sc in next dc, skip next dc, shell in next sc, skip next dc) around, join, fasten off (8 shells, 8 sc).

Rnd 5: Join green with sc in 3rd dc of any shell, *ch 2, skip next 2 dc, (dc, ch 1, dc) in next sc, ch 2, skip next 2 dc*, [sc in next dc; repeat between **]; repeat between [ ] around, join, fasten off (16 dc, 16 ch-2 sps, 8 sc, 8 ch-1 sps).

Rnd 6: Join yellow with sc in any sc, 2 sc in each ch-2 sp, sc in each ch-1 sp and sc in each st around, join (64 sc).

Rnd 7: Ch 4, (tr, ch 2, 2 tr) in same st, *dc in each of next 2 sts, hdc in each of next 2 sts, sc in next 7 sts, hdc in each of next 2 sts, dc in each of next 2 sts*, [(2 tr, ch 2, 2 tr) in next st; repeat between **]; repeat between [ ] around, join with sl st in top of ch-4 (28 sc, 16 tr, 16 dc, 16 hdc, 4 ch-2 sps).

Rnd 8: Ch 1, sc in each st around with (sc, ch 2, sc) in each ch-2 sp, join with sl st in first sc, fasten off (84 sc, 4 ch-2 sps).

Rnd 9: Join brown with sc in any ch-2 sp, ch 3, sc in same sp, *ch 1, skip next st, (sc in next st, ch 1, skip next st) 10 times*, [(sc, ch 3, sc) in next st; repeat between **]; repeat between [ ] around, join, fasten off (48 sc, 44 ch-1 sps, 4 ch-3 sps).

With brown, sew Blocks together in eight rows of six Blocks each.

Edging

Rnd 1: Join brown with sl st in ch sp on top right corner, ch 1, [(sc, ch 2, sc) in same sp, *sc in next st, (sc in next ch sp, sc in next st) 11 times, hdc in next ch sp, dc in next seam, hdc in next ch sp*; repeat between ** 4 more times, sc in next st, (sc in next ch sp, sc in next st) 11 times, (sc, ch 2, sc) in next ch sp; repeat between

** 7 more times, (sc in next ch sp, sc in next st) 11 times]; repeat between [ ] one more time, join with sl st in first sc (652 sc, 48 hdc, 24 dc, 4 ch-2 sps).

Rnd 2: Ch 1, sc in each st around with (sc, ch 2, sc) in each ch-2 sp, join, fasten off (732 sc, 4 ch-2 sps).

Rnd 3: Join yellow with sc in first ch-2 sp, ch 2, sc in same sp, *ch 1, skip next st, (sc in next st, ch 1, skip next st) across to next ch-2 sp*, [(sc, ch 2, sc) in next sp; repeat between **]; repeat between [ ] around, join (372 sc, 368 ch-1 sps, 4 ch-2 sps).

Rnd 4: Ch 3, dc in each st and in each ch-1 sp around with (2 dc, ch 2, 2 dc) in each ch-2 sp, join with sl st in top of ch-3, **turn** (756 dc, 4 ch-2 sps).

Rnd 5: Sl st in next st, ch 1, sc in same st, *ch 1, (skip next st, sc in next st, ch 1) across to next ch-2 sp, (sc, ch 2, sc) in next ch-2 sp*; repeat between ** 3 times, ch 1, skip next st, sc in next st, ch 1, skip last st, join, **turn** (384 sc, 380 ch-1 sps, 4 ch-2 sps).

Rnd 6: Ch 3, dc in each st and in each ch-1 sp around with (2 dc, ch 2, 2 dc) in each ch-2 sp, join with sl st in top of ch-3, **do not** turn, fasten off (780 dc, 4 ch-2 sps).

Rnd 7: Join dk. yellow with sc in ch-2 sp on top right corner, ch 2, sc in same sp, *ch 1, skip next st, (sc in next st, ch 1, skip next st) across to next ch-2 sp*, [(sc, ch 2, sc) in next sp; repeat between **]; repeat between [ ] around, join with sl st in first sc, **turn** (396 sc, 392 ch-1 sps, 4 ch-2 sps).

Rnd 8: Ch 1, sc in each st and in each ch-1 sp around with (sc, ch 2, sc) in each ch-2 sp, join, **turn** (796 sc, 4 ch-2 sps).

Rnd 9: Sl st in next st, (sl st, ch 3, 4 dc) in next ch-2 sp, *skip next st, sc in next st, (skip next 2 sts, shell in next st, skip next 2 sts, sc in next st) across to one st before next ch-2 sp, skip next st, shell in next ch-2 sp, skip next 2 sts, sc in next st, (skip next 2 sts, shell in next st, skip next 2 sts, sc in next st) across to 2 sts before next ch-2 sp, skip next 2 sts*, [shell in next ch-2 sp; repeat between **]; repeat between [ ] around, join, **turn,** fasten off (134 shells, 134 sc).

Rnd 10: Join green with sc in center dc of shell on top right corner, ch 2, sc in same dc, sc in each st around with (sc, ch 2, sc) in center dc of each shell, join, **do not** turn (938 sc, 134 ch-2 sps).

Rnd 11: *(Sl st, ch 3, sl st, ch 3, sl st, ch 3, sl st) in corner ch-2 sp, ch 3, skip next 3 sts, (sl st, ch 3, sl st) in next st, ch 3, skip next 3 sts, (sl st, ch 3, sl st) in next ch-2 sp, ◊ ch 3, skip next 3 sts, sl st in next st, ch 3, skip next 3 sts, (sl st, ch 3, sl st) in next ch-2 sp; repeat from ◊ across to last 7 sts before corner ch-2 sp, ch 3, skip next 3 sts, (sl st, ch 3, sl st) in next st, ch 3, skip next 3 sts; repeat from * around, join with sl st in first sl st, fasten off.∞

Medallion Ripple

by designer Sandra Smith

Two perennial favorites — motifs and ripples — are combined in this clever afghan. Country colors of blue, yellow and brown create a warm and cozy look.

Medallion Ripple

Finished Size

48" x 68".

Materials

Worsted-weight yarn — 42 oz. taupe, 21 oz. yellow, and 8 oz. blue; tapestry needle; F crochet hook or size needed to obtain gauge.

Gauge

Medallion is 4" x 4½"; 11 sc **back lp** rows = 3".
   Note: Afghan may ruffle slightly until blocked.

Skill Level

★★ Average

Instructions

Whole Medallion (make 104)

   Rnd 1: With blue, ch 2, 6 sc in 2nd ch from hook, join with sl st in first sc, fasten off (6 sc).

   Rnd 2: Join yellow with sl st in first st, ch 3, 2 dc in same st, ch 2, (3 dc in next st, ch 2) around, join with sl st in top of ch-3, fasten off (18 dc, 6 ch-2 sps).

   Rnd 3: Join blue with sc in first ch sp, ch 2, sc in same sp, sc in each of next 3 sts, *(sc, ch 2, sc) in next ch sp, sc in each of next 3 sts; repeat from * around, join with sl st in first sc, fasten off (30 sc, 6 ch sps).

   Rnd 4: Join yellow with sl st in first ch sp, ch 5, dc in same sp, dc in next 5 sts; *for **V-stitch (V-st)** *(see fig. 25, page 158),* **(dc, ch 2, dc) in next ch sp;** dc in next 5 sts; repeat from * around, join with sl st in 3rd ch of ch-5, fasten off (30 dc, 6 V-sts).

   Rnd 5: Join taupe with sc in first ch sp, ch 2, sc in same sp, sc in next 7 sts, *(sc, ch 2, sc) in next V-st, sc in next 7 sts; repeat from * around, join with sl st in first sc, fasten off (54 sc, 6 ch sps).

Half Medallion (make 8)

   Row 1: With blue, ch 2, 3 sc in 2nd ch from hook, **do not** turn, fasten off (3 sc).

   Row 2: Join yellow with sl st in first st, ch 3, 2 dc in same st, (ch 2, 3 dc in next st) across, **do not** turn, fasten off (9 dc, 2 ch sps).

   Row 3: Join blue with sc in first st, sc in same st, sc in each of next 2 sts, (sc, ch 2, sc) in next ch sp, sc in each of next 3 sts, (sc, ch 2, sc) in next ch sp, sc in each of next 2 sts, 2 sc in last st, **do not** turn, fasten off (15 sc, 2 ch sps).

   Row 4: Join yellow with sl st in first st, ch 3, dc in same st, dc in next 4 sts, V-st, dc in next 5 sts, V-st, dc in next 4 sts, 2 dc in last st, **do not** turn, fasten off (21 dc, 2 V-sts).

   Rnd 5: Working in rnds, join taupe with sc in first st, (ch 2, sc) in same st, sc in next 6 sts, (sc, ch 2, sc) in next ch sp, sc in next 7 sts, (sc, ch 2, sc) in next ch sp, sc in next 6 sts, (sc, ch 2, sc) in last st; working in ends of rows, (2 sc in next row, sc in next row) 2 times, (sc in next row, 2 sc in next row) 2 times, join with sl st in first sc, fasten off (39 sc, 4 ch sps).

Center Section

   Using 34 whole medallions and four half medallions, holding right sides together, matching sts and chs, working in **back lps** *(see fig. 1, page 154),* sl st together according to Placement Diagram A on page 17, fasten off.

First Half of Afghan
Center Ripple Section

   Row 1: Working these rows in **back lps,** join taupe with sc in 2nd ch of first corner (see Diagram A) on first half medallion, sc in next 8 sts, skip next

2 ch sps, sc in next 9 sts, (sc in next ch, ch 2, sc in next ch, sc in next 9 sts, skip next 2 ch sps, sc in next 9 sts) 11 times, turn (238 sc, 11 ch sps).

Rows 2-9: Ch 1, 2 sc in first st, sc in next 7 sts, skip next 2 sts, (sc in next 9 sts, sc in next ch, ch 2, sc in next ch, sc in next 9 sts, skip next 2 sts) 11 times, sc in next 7 sts, 2 sc in last st, turn. Fasten off at end of last row.

Row 10: Join yellow with sc in first st, sc in same st, sc in next 7 sts, skip next 2 sts, (sc in next 9 sts, sc in next ch, ch 2, sc in next ch, sc in next 9 sts, skip next 2 sts) 11 times, sc in next 7 sts, 2 sc in last st, turn.

Row 11: Repeat row 2.

Row 12: With taupe, repeat row 10.

Rows 13-15: Repeat row 2.

Rows 16-17: With blue, repeat rows 10 and 11.

Row 18: With taupe, repeat row 10.

Rows 19-25: Repeat row 2.

End Medallion Section

Using 35 whole medallions and two half medallions, holding right sides together, matching sts and chs, sl st **back lps** together according to Placement Diagram B at right.

Holding right sides together, matching sts and chs, sl st **back lps** of End Medallion Section and Center Ripple Section together, fasten off.

End Ripple Section

Row 1: Working these rows in **back lps,** join taupe with sc in first st (see Diagram B), sc in next 8 sts, (sc in next ch, ch 2, sc in next ch, sc in next 9 sts, skip next 2 ch sps), *sc in next 9 sts; repeat between ( ); repeat from * across, turn (240 sc, 12 ch sps).

Rows 2-9: Ch 1, sc first 2 sts tog, sc in next 8 sts, sc in next ch, ch 2, sc in next ch, (sc in next 9 sts,

skip next 2 sts, sc in next 9 sts, sc in next ch, ch 2, sc in next ch) 11 times, sc in next 8 sts, sc last 2 sts tog, turn. Fasten off at end of last row.

Row 10: Join yellow with sl st in first st, ch 1, sc first 2 sts tog, sc in next 8 sts, sc in next ch, ch 2, sc in next ch, (sc in next 9 sts, skip next 2 sts, sc in next 9 sts, sc in next ch, ch 2, sc in next ch) 11 times, sc in next 8 sts, sc last 2 sts tog, turn.

Row 11: Repeat row 2.

Row 12: With taupe, repeat row 10.

Rows 13-15: Repeat row 2.

Rows 16-17: With blue, repeat rows 10 and 11.

Rows 18-19: With taupe, repeat rows 10 and 11.

Second Half of Afghan

Repeat First Half of Afghan on opposite side of Center Medallion Section.∞

PLACEMENT DIAGRAM A

Join here for
First Half of Afghan

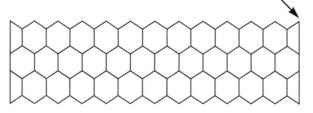

PLACEMENT DIAGRAM B

Join here for
End Ripple Section

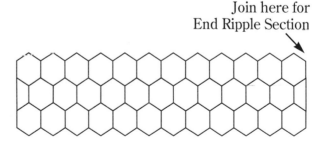

Coral Waves

by designer Dorris Brooks

Select three shades of your favorite color to make a classically-styled and easy-to-make afghan that's pure crocheting pleasure, row by row.

Finished Size

46" x 75" without fringe.

Materials

Worsted-weight yarn — 17 oz. dk. peach, 13 oz. each med. peach and lt. peach; tapestry needle; I crochet hook or size needed to obtain gauge.

Gauge

3 dc sts = 1", 1 shell = 1¾" across; 3 dc rows = 2".

Skill Level

★ Easy

Instructions

Afghan

Row 1: With dk. peach, ch 139, sc in 2nd ch from hook, sc in next 4 chs, ch 2, skip next 2 chs, (sc in next 7 chs, ch 2, skip next 2 chs) across with sc in last 5 chs, turn (108 sc, 15 ch sps).

Note: For **shell,** (2 dc, ch 2, 2 dc, ch 2, 2 dc) in next ch-2 sp.

Row 2: Ch 3, dc in each of next 2 sts, *skip next 2 sts, shell in next ch sp, skip next 2 sts, dc in each of next 3 sts; repeat from * across, turn (48 dc, 15 shells).

Row 3: Ch 3, dc in each of next 2 sts, *ch 2, sc in first ch sp of next shell, ch 2, sc in 2nd ch sp of same shell, ch 2, skip last 2 dc of same shell, dc in each of next 3 sts; repeat from * across, turn (48 dc, 45 ch sps).

Rows 4-6: Repeat rows 2 and 3 alternately, ending with row 2. Fasten off at end of last row.

Row 7: Join med. peach with sl st in first st, repeat row 3.

Rows 8-114: Repeat rows 2-7 consecutively, working in color sequence of lt. peach, dk. peach and med. peach, ending with row 6. **Do not** fasten off at end of last row.

Row 115: Ch 3, dc in each of next 2 sts, *ch 2, sc in first ch sp of next shell, sc in each of next 2 sts of same shell, sc in 2nd ch sp of same shell, ch 2, skip last 2 sts of same shell, dc in each of next 3 sts; repeat from * across, fasten off.

Fringe

For **each fringe,** cut three strands of dk. peach each 16" long. With all three strands held together, fold in half, insert hook in stitch, draw fold through, draw all loose ends through fold, tighten. Trim ends.

Fringe in every other stitch or chain space on short ends of afghan.∞

Romantic Lace

Elegant patterns and old-fashioned
colors bring to mind a bygone era when
needlework for enjoyment, not necessity,
was the pastime of ladies of privilege.
Capture the look of Victorian romance
in traditional pineapples, lace-trimmed
florals, or delicate stripes.

Pink Diamonds

by designer Rose Pirrone

Stripes and diamonds are combined in an unusual pattern in this warm and lush textured throw. It's the perfect companion for an evening of reading or movie-watching.

Finished Size

56" x 76".

Materials

Worsted-weight yarn — 46 oz. lt. pink and 34 oz. dk. pink; tapestry needle; G crochet hook or size needed to obtain gauge.

Gauge

4 sc sts = 1"; 4 sc rows = 1".

Skill Level

★★ Average

Instructions

Afghan

Row 1: With lt. pink, ch 213, sc in 2nd ch from hook, sc in each ch across, turn (212).

Row 2: Ch 1, sc in each st across, turn.

Note: Ch-3 at beginning of each row counts as first st.

Rows 3-4: Ch 3, dc in each of next 2 sts, *skip next 2 sts, tr in each of next 2 sts; working behind 2 tr just made, tr in each skipped st, skip next 2 sts, tr in each of next 2 sts; working in **front** of 2 tr just made, tr in each skipped st, dc in each of next 3 sts; repeat from * across, turn.

Rows 5-6: Ch 1, sc in each st across, turn.

Rows 7-14: Repeat rows 3-6 consecutively. Fasten off at end of last row.

Row 15: Join dk. pink with sc in first st, sc in each st across, turn.

Row 16: Ch 1, sc in each st across, turn.

Rows 17-24: Repeat rows 3-6 consecutively. Fasten off at end of last row.

Row 25: Join lt. pink with sc in first st, sc in each st across, turn.

Row 26: Ch 1, sc in each st across, turn.

Rows 27-38: Repeat rows 3-6 consecutively. Fasten off at end of last row.

Rows 39-206: Repeat rows 15-38 consecutively.

Border

Rnd 1: Join dk. pink with sc in any corner, 2 sc in same sp, sc in end of each sc row, 2 sc in end of each dc row and sc in each st around with 3 sc in each corner, join with sl st in first sc (892).

Rnd 2: Ch 1, sc in same st, (ch 4, skip next st, sc in next st) around to last st, skip last st; to **join,** ch 1, dc in first sc (446 ch lps).

Rnd 3: Ch 5, dc over dc just made, ch 1, sc in next ch lp, ch 1, *(dc, ch 2, dc) in next ch lp, ch 1, sc in next ch lp, ch 1; repeat from * around, join with sl st in 3rd ch of ch-5, fasten off. ∞

Victorian Flower Garden

by designer Dorris Brooks

Bring all the bounty of a Victorian perennial garden into your home with this lacy, floral afghan. Square motifs set on point are crocheted together as you work.

Finished Size

51" x 71".

Materials

Worsted-weight yarn — 17 oz. off-white, 13 oz. each lt. teal and dk. teal, 4 oz. yellow, small amount each seven assorted flower colors; tapestry needle; I crochet hook or size needed to obtain gauge.

Gauge

Rnd 1 = 2" across.

Skill Level

★ Easy

Instructions

Block No. 1

Rnd 1: With yellow, ch 4, 3 dc in 4th ch from hook, ch 2, (4 dc, ch 2) 3 times in same ch, join with sl st in top of ch-3, fasten off (16 dc, 4 ch sps).

Rnd 2: Join flower color with sl st in any ch sp, ch 4, 6 tr in same sp, skip next 2 dc, sc in next dc, *7 tr in next ch sp, skip next 2 dc, sc in next dc; repeat from * around, join with sl st in top of ch-4, fasten off (28 tr, 4 sc).

Notes: For **beginning shell (beg shell)**, ch 3, (2 dc, ch 2, 3 dc) in same st or sp.

For **V-stitch (V-st)** *(see fig. 25, page 158),* (dc, ch 1, dc) in next st or sp.

For **shell** *(see fig. 22, page 157),* (3 dc, ch 2, 3 dc) in next st or sp.

Rnd 3: Join lt. teal with sl st in 4th tr of any 7-tr group, beg shell, *ch 1, skip next 3 tr, V-st in next sc, ch 1, skip next 3 tr*, [shell in next tr; repeat between **]; repeat between [ ] around, join with sl st in top of ch-3, fasten off (8 ch-1 sps, 4 shells, 4 V-sts).

Rnd 4: Join dk. teal with sl st in ch sp of any shell, beg shell, *skip next 2 dc of same shell, V-st in next dc, V-st in ch sp of next V-st, skip last dc of same V-st, V-st in first dc of next shell*, [shell in ch sp of same shell; repeat between **]; repeat between [ ] around, join, fasten off (12 V-sts, 4 shells).

Rnd 5: Join off-white with sc in ch sp of any shell, (sc, ch 2, 2 sc) in same sp, sc in each dc and in each ch-1 sp around with (2 sc, ch 2, 2 sc) in ch-2 sp of each shell, join with sl st in first sc (76 sc, 4 ch-2 sps).

Rnd 6: Ch 1, sc in same st, ch 3, skip next sc, (sc, ch 3, sc) in next ch-2 sp, *ch 3, skip next sc, (sc in next sc, ch 3, skip next sc) across to next ch-2 sp, (sc, ch 3, sc) in next ch-2 sp; repeat from * around to last 17 sc, ch 3, skip next sc, (sc in next sc, ch 3, skip next sc) around, join, fasten off (44 ch lps).

Block Nos. 2-59

Notes: For **joining ch lp,** ch 1, sl st in ch lp on next motif, ch 1.

Join motifs together according to diagram on this page.

Rnds 1-5: Repeat same rnds of Block No. 1 on page 25.

Rnd 6: Repeat same rnd of Block No. 1 using joining ch lp when joining motifs.

Border

Rnd 1: Join off-white with sc in any corner ch lp, ch 3, sc in same lp, ch 3, (sc in next ch lp or in joining sl st, ch 3) around with (sc, ch 3) 2 times in each corner ch lp, join with sl st in first sc.

Rnd 2: Sl st in first ch lp, ch 1, (sc, ch 3, sc) in same lp, ch 3, (sc in next ch lp, ch 3) around with (sc, ch 3) 2 times in each corner ch lp, join, fasten off.∽

JOINING DIAGRAM

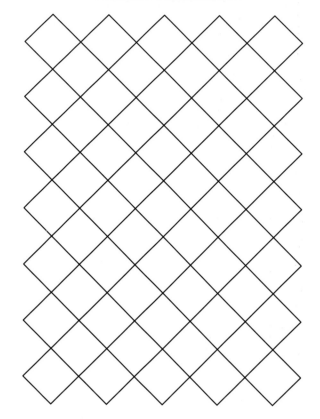

Wildflowers & Lace

by designer Joan Drost

This delicate, yet dazzling afghan is as soft as a flower petal. Each motif can be completed in just a few minutes, making this a great summer take-along project.

Wildflowers & Lace

Finished Size

47" x 63".

Materials

2-ply fuzzy bulky-weight yarn — 30 oz. white, 17 oz. pink, white and yellow multicolor, 2 oz. pink and 1 oz. yellow; tapestry needle; G crochet hook or size needed to obtain gauge.

Gauge

Rnds 1-2 of Small Square = 3".

Skill Level

★★ Average

Instructions

Small Square (make 82)

Rnd 1: With white, ch 5, sl st in first ch to form ring, ch 1, 12 sc in ring, join with sl st in first sc (12).

Note: For **double treble crochet (dtr)** *(see fig. 8, page 155),* yo 3 times, insert hook in next st, yo, draw lp through, (yo, draw through 2 lps on hook) 4 times.

Rnd 2: (Ch 11, sl st in next st) around; to **join,** ch 6, dtr in bottom of first ch-11 (12 ch lps).

Rnd 3: Ch 1, sc over joining dtr just made, ch 3, sc in next ch lp, ch 3; for **corner, (2 dc, ch 2, 2 dc) in next ch lp;** ch 3, *(sc in next ch lp, ch 3) 2 times, corner, ch 3; repeat from * around, join with sl st in first sc (12 ch-3 sps, 4 corners).

Rnd 4: Sl st into first ch-3 sp, ch 3, dc in same sp, *ch 3, sc in next ch-3 sp, ch 3, corner in next corner ch-2 sp, ch 3, sc in next ch-3 sp, ch 3*, [2 dc in next ch-3 sp; repeat between **]; repeat between [ ] around, join with sl st in top of ch-3, fasten off (16 ch-3 sps, 8 dc, 4 corners).

Large Square (make 12)

Rnd 1: With yellow, ch 2, 8 sc in 2nd ch from hook, join with sl st in first sc (8).

Rnd 2: Ch 1, sc in each st around, join, fasten off.

Rnd 3: Join pink with sl st in any st; for **petal, ch 7, sc in 2nd ch from hook, hdc in next ch, dc in each of next 2 chs, hdc in next ch, sc in last ch;** (sl st in next st on rnd 2, petal) around, join with sl st in first sl st, fasten off (8 petals, 8 sl sts).

Rnd 4: Working behind petals, join white with sl st in any sl st, ch 7, (dc in next sl st, ch 4) around, join with sl st in 3rd ch of ch-7 (8 ch-4 sps).

Rnd 5: Ch 3, 4 dc in first ch sp, ch 3, skip next st, 4 dc in next ch sp, *dc in next st, 4 dc in next ch sp, ch 3, skip next st, 4 dc in next ch sp; repeat from * around, join with sl st in top of ch-3 (36 dc, 4 ch-3 sps).

Rnd 6: Ch 1; to join petals to square, working through both thicknesses, sc in tip of next petal and in first st, *working in rnd 5 **only,** sc in next 4 sts, 3 sc in next ch-3 sp, (working through both thicknesses, sc in tip of next petal and in next st), working in rnd 5 **only,** sc in each of next 3 sts*; [repeat between ( ); repeat between **]; repeat between [ ] around, join with sl st in first sc, fasten off (48 sc).

Rnd 7: Join multicolor with sl st in center st of any 3-sc corner; for **beginning corner (beg corner), (ch 3, dc, ch 2, 2 dc)** in same st; ch 1, skip next st, (2 dc in next st, ch

1, skip next st) 5 times, *corner in next st, ch 1, skip next st, (2 dc in next st, ch 1, skip next st) 5 times; repeat from * around, join (24 ch-1 sps, 4 corners).

Rnds 8-11: Sl st in next st, sl st into first ch-2 sp, beg corner, ch 1, (2 dc in next ch-1 sp, ch 1) around to next corner, *corner in next corner ch-2 sp, ch 1, (2 dc in next ch-1 sp, ch 1) around to next corner; repeat from * around, join, ending with 40 ch-1 sps and 4 corners in last rnd. Fasten off at end of last rnd.

Sew Small and Large Squares together according to diagram below.

Border

Rnd 1: With right side of afghan facing you, join multicolor with sl st in any corner ch-2 sp, (ch 2, hdc, ch 2, 2 hdc) in same sp, ch 2, (2 hdc in next ch sp, ch 2) around to next corner ch-2 sp, *(2 hdc, ch 2, 2 hdc) in next corner ch-2 sp, ch 2, (2 hdc in next ch sp, ch 2) around to next corner ch-2 sp; repeat from * around, join with sl st in top of ch-2, fasten off.

Rnd 2: Join white with sl st in any ch sp, ch 5, (sl st in next ch sp, ch 5) around, join with sl st in first sl st, fasten off.

ASSEMBLY DIAGRAM

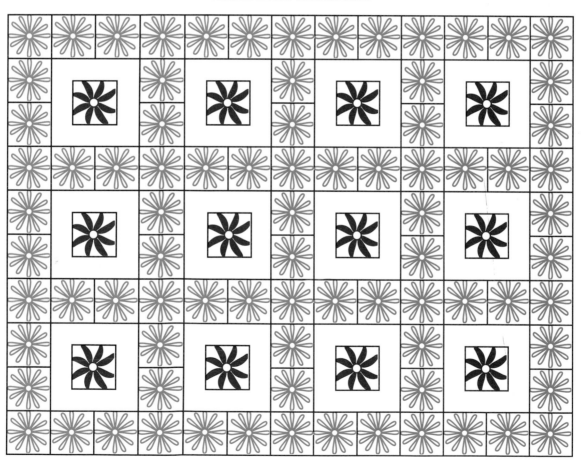

English Country
by designer Diane Simpson

Easy post stitches form a beautiful textured pattern for this generous-size afghan.

Finished Size
50½" x 70½" not including fringe.

Materials
Worsted-weight yarn — 39½ oz. white, 16 oz. each apricot and turquoise; tapestry needle; I crochet hook or size needed to obtain gauge.

Gauge
3 pattern rows = 2".

Skill Level
★★ Average

Instructions

Afghan

Note: For **V-stitch (V-st)** *(see fig. 25, page 158),* (dc, ch 3, dc) in next ch or ch-3 sp.

Row 1: With white, ch 224, dc in 6th ch from hook, dc in each of next 2 chs, V-st, dc in each of next 3 chs, *skip next 4 chs, dc in each of next 3 chs, V-st, dc in each of next 3 chs; repeat from * across to last 3 chs, skip next 2 chs, dc in last ch, turn (122 dc, 20 V-sts).

Note: For **front post stitch (fp)** *(see fig. 23, page 158),* yo, insert hook from front to back around post of st on previous row, complete as dc.

Row 2: Ch 3, skip next st, *fp around next st, bp around next st, fp around next st, V-st, fp around next st, bp around next st, fp around next st*, [skip next 2 sts; repeat between **]; repeat between [ ] 18 times, skip next st, dc in last st, turn, fasten off (80 fp, 40 bp, 20 V-sts, 2 dc).

Row 3: Join apricot with sl st in first st, ch 3, skip next fp, *bp around next bp, fp around next fp, bp around next dc, V-st, bp around next dc, fp around next fp, bp around next bp*, [skip next 2 fp; repeat between **]; repeat between [ ] 18 times, skip next st, dc in last st, turn.

Row 4: Ch 3, skip next bp, *fp around next fp, bp around next bp, fp around next dc, V-st, fp around next fp, bp around next bp, fp around next fp*, [skip next 2 bp; repeat between **]; repeat between [ ] 18 times, skip next st, dc in last st, turn, fasten off.

Row 5: With white, repeat row 3.

Row 6: Ch 3, skip next bp, *fp around next fp, bp around next bp, fp around next dc, V-st, fp around next fp, bp around next bp, fp around next fp*, [skip next 2 bp; repeat between **]; repeat between [ ] 18 times, skip next st, dc in last st, turn, fasten off.

Row 7: With turquoise, repeat row 3.

Row 8: Ch 3, skip next bp, *fp around next fp, bp around next bp, fp around next dc, V-st, fp around next fp, bp around next bp, fp around next fp*, [skip next 2 bp; repeat between **]; repeat between [ ] 18 times, skip next st, dc in last st, turn, fasten off.

Row 9: Repeat row 3.

Rows 10-106: Repeat rows 2-9 consecutively, ending with row 2.

Fringe

For **each fringe,** cut three strands white each 14" long. With all three strands held together, fold in half, insert hook in st, draw fold through, draw all loose ends through fold, tighten. Trim ends.

Fringe in every other st and in each ch sp on short ends of afghan.∽

Pineapple Perfection

by designer Dorothy Myers

Decorate a sunny bedroom with the welcoming beauty of pineapples. Large enough to cover a twin-sized bed, this afghan is gorgeous in any color.

Finished Size

49" x 81".

Materials

Worsted-weight yarn — 56 oz. yellow; tapestry needle; G crochet hook or size needed to obtain gauge.

Gauge

One shell *(see notes)* = 1¼" across; one shell row = 1".

Skill Level

★★ Average

Instructions

Motif (make 7)

Notes: For **beginning shell (beg shell),** ch 3, (dc, ch 2, 2 dc) in same sp.

For **shell** *(see fig. 22, page 157),* (2 dc, ch 2, 2 dc) in next ch sp.

For **V-stitch (V-st)** *(see fig. 25, page 158),* (dc, ch 3, dc) in next st.

Row 1: Ch 4, (dc, ch 3, 2 dc) in 4th ch from hook, turn (4 dc, 1 ch sp).

Row 2: Ch 1, sl st in first 2 dc, sl st in first ch sp, ch 3, (dc, ch 2, 2 dc, ch 2, 2 dc) in same sp, turn (6 dc).

Row 3: Ch 1, sl st in first 2 dc, sl st in first ch sp, beg shell, shell in last ch sp, turn (2 shells).

Row 4: Ch 1, sl st in first 2 dc, sl st in first ch sp, beg shell, dc in next sp between shells, shell in last shell, turn (2 shells, 1 dc).

Row 5: Ch 1, sl st in first 2 dc, sl st in first ch sp, beg shell, ch 1, skip last 2 dc of same shell, V-st in next dc, ch 1, shell in last shell, turn (2 shells, 2 ch-1 sps, 1 V-st).

Row 6: Ch 1, sl st in first 2 dc, sl st in first ch sp, beg shell, ch 1, 9 dc in ch sp of next V-st, ch 1, shell in last shell, turn.

Row 7: Ch 1, sl st in first 2 dc, sl st in first ch sp, beg shell, ch 1, skip last 2 dc of same shell, dc in next dc, (ch 1, dc in next dc) 8 times, ch 1, shell in last shell, turn.

Row 8: Ch 1, sl st in first 2 dc, sl st in first ch sp, beg shell, ch 3, skip next ch-1 sp, (sc in next ch-1 sp, ch 3) 8 times, skip next ch-1 sp, shell in last shell, turn, fasten off. **Do not** fasten off at end of last row on last motif made.

Afghan

Row 1: Ch 1, sl st in first 2 dc, sl st in first ch sp, beg shell, *ch 3, skip next ch-3 sp, (sc in next ch-3 sp, ch 3) 7 times, skip next ch-3 sp, shell in last shell, **do not** turn*; [to **join next motif,** with wrong side of row 8 facing you, shell in first shell; repeat between **]; repeat between [ ] until all motifs are joined, **turn** (56 ch-3 sps, 14 shells).

Row 2: Ch 1, sl st in first 2 dc, sl st in first ch sp, beg shell, *ch 3, skip next ch-3 sp, (sc in next ch-3 sp, ch 3) 6 times, skip next ch-3 sp*, [shell in each of next 2 shells; repeat between **]; repeat between [ ] across with shell in last shell, turn (49 ch-3 sps, 14 shells).

Row 3: Ch 1, sl st in first 2 dc, sl st in first ch sp, beg shell, *ch 3, skip next ch-3 sp, (sc in next ch-3 sp, ch 3) 5 times, skip next ch-3 sp, shell in next shell*, [dc in next space between shells, shell in next shell; repeat between **]; repeat between [ ] across, turn (42 ch-3 sps, 14 shells, 6 dc).

Row 4: Ch 1, sl st in first 2 dc, sl st in first ch sp, beg shell, *ch 3, skip next ch-3 sp, (sc in next ch-3 sp, ch 3) 4 times, skip next ch-3 sp, shell in next shell*, [ch 1, skip last 2 dc of same shell, V-st in next dc, ch 1, shell in next shell; repeat between **]; repeat between [ ] across, turn (35 ch-3 sps, 14 shells, 12 ch-1 sps, 6 V-sts).

Row 5: Ch 1, sl st in first 2 dc, sl st in first ch sp, beg shell, *ch 3, skip next ch-3 sp, (sc in next ch-3 sp, ch 3) 3 times, skip next ch-3 sp, shell in next shell*, [ch 1, 9 dc in next V-st, ch 1, shell in next shell; repeat between **]; repeat between [ ] across, turn (54 dc, 28 ch-2 sps, 14 shells, 12 ch-1 sps).

Row 6: Ch 1, sl st in first 2 dc, sl st in first ch sp, beg shell, *ch 3, skip next ch-3 sp, (sc in next ch-3 sp, ch 3) 2 times, skip next ch-3 sp, shell in next shell*, [ch 1, skip last 2 dc of same shell, (dc in next dc, ch 1) 9 times, shell in next shell; repeat between **]; repeat between [ ] across, turn (60 ch-1 sps, 21 ch-3 sps, 14 shells).

Row 7: Ch 1, sl st in first 2 dc, sl st in first ch sp, beg shell, *ch 3, skip next ch-3 sp, sc in next ch-3 sp, ch 3, skip next ch-3 sp, shell in next shell*, [ch 3, skip next ch-1 sp, (sc in next ch-1 sp, ch 3) 8 times, skip next ch-1 sp, shell in next shell; repeat between **]; repeat between [ ] across, turn (68 ch-3 sps).

Row 8: Ch 1, sl st in first 2 dc, sl st in first ch sp, beg shell, skip next 2 ch-3 sps, shell in next shell, *ch 3, skip next ch-3 sp, (sc in next ch-3 sp, ch 3) 7 times, skip next ch-3 sp, shell in next shell, skip next 2 ch-3 sps, shell in next shell; repeat from * across, turn (48 ch-3 sps).

Row 9: Ch 1, sl st in first 2 dc, sl st in first ch sp, beg shell, shell in next shell, *ch 3, skip next ch-3 sp, (sc in next ch-3 sp, ch 3) 6 times, skip next ch-3 sp, shell in each of next 2 shells; repeat from * across, turn (42 ch-3 sps, 14 shells).

Row 10: Ch 1, sl st in first 2 dc, sl st in first ch sp, beg shell, dc in next sp between shells, shell in next shell, *ch 3, skip next ch-3 sp, (sc in next ch-3 sp, ch 3) 5 times, skip next ch-3 sp, shell in next shell, dc in next sp between shells, shell in next shell; repeat from * across, turn (36 ch-3 sps, 7 dc).

Row 11: Ch 1, sl st in first 2 dc, sl st in first ch sp, beg shell, *ch 1, skip last 2 dc of same shell, V-st in next dc, ch 1, shell in next shell*, [ch 3, skip next ch-3 sp, (sc in next ch-3 sp, ch 3) 4 times, shell in next shell; repeat between **]; repeat between [ ] across, turn (30 ch-3 sps, 14 shells, 14 ch-1 sps, 7 V-sts).

Row 12: Ch 1, sl st in first 2 dc, sl st in first ch sp, beg shell, *ch 1, 9 dc in next V-st, ch 1, shell in next shell*, [ch 3, skip next ch-3 sp, (sc in next ch-3 sp, ch 3) 3 times, skip next ch-3 sp, shell in next shell; repeat between **]; repeat between [ ] across, turn (63 dc, 24 ch-3 sps, 14 shells, 14 ch-1 sps).

Row 13: Ch 1, sl st in first 2 dc, sl st in first ch sp, beg shell, *ch 1, skip last 2 dc of same shell, (dc in next dc, ch 1) 9 times, shell in next shell*, [ch 3, skip next ch-3 sp, (sc in next ch-3 sp, ch 3) 2 times, skip next ch-3 sp, shell in next shell; repeat between **]; repeat between [ ] across, turn (70 ch-1 sps, 18 ch-3 sps, 14 shells).

Row 14: Ch 1, sl st in first 2 dc, sl st in first ch sp, beg shell, *ch 3, skip next ch-1 sp, (sc in next ch-1 sp, ch 3) 8 times, shell in next shell*, [ch 3, skip next ch-3 sp, sc in next ch-3 sp, ch 3, skip next ch-3 sp, shell in next shell; repeat between **]; repeat between [ ] across, turn (75 ch-3 sps, 14 shells).

Row 15: Ch 1, sl st in first 2 dc, sl st in first ch sp, beg shell, *ch 3, skip next ch-3 sp, (sc in next ch-3 sp, ch 3) 7 times, skip next ch-3 sp, shell in next shell*, [skip next 2 ch-3 sps, shell in next shell; repeat between **]; repeat between [ ] across, turn (56 ch-3 sps, 14 shells).

Rows 16-128: Repeat rows 2-15 consecutively, ending with row 2.

Row 129: For **first point,** ch 1, sl st in first 2 dc, sl st in first ch sp, beg shell, ch 3, skip next ch-3 sp, (sc in next ch-3 sp, ch 3) 5 times, skip next ch-3 sp, shell in next shell leaving remaining sts unworked, turn (6 ch-3 sps).

Row 130: Ch 1, sl st in first 2 dc, sl st in first ch sp, beg shell, ch 3, skip next ch-3 sp, (sc in next ch-3 sp, ch 3) 4 times, skip next ch-3 sp, shell in last shell, turn (5 ch-3 sps, 2 shells).

Row 131: Ch 1, sl st in first 2 dc, sl st in first ch sp, beg shell, ch 3, skip next ch-3 sp, (sc in next ch-3 sp, ch 3) 3 times, skip next ch-3 sp, shell in last shell, turn (4 ch-3 sps, 2 shells).

Row 132: Ch 1, sl st in first 2 dc, sl st in first ch sp, beg shell, ch 3, skip next ch-3 sp, (sc in next ch-3 sp, ch 3) 2 times, skip next ch-3 sp, shell in last shell, turn (3 ch-3 sps, 2 shells).

Row 133: Ch 1, sl st in first 2 dc, sl st in first ch sp, beg shell, ch 3, skip next ch-3 sp, sc in next ch-3 sp, ch 3, skip next ch-3 sp, shell in last shell, turn (2 shells, 2 ch-3 sps).

Row 134: Ch 1, sl st in first 2 dc, sl st in first ch sp, beg shell, skip next 2 ch-3 sps, shell in last shell, turn.

Row 135: Ch 1, sl st in first 2 dc, sl st in first ch sp, ch 3, dc in same sp, ch 2, 2 dc in next sp between shells, ch 2, 2 dc in last shell, turn.

Row 136: Ch 1, sl st in first 2 dc, sl st in first ch sp, ch 3, dc in same sp, ch 2, 2 dc in last ch sp, turn.

Row 137: Ch 1, sl st in first 2 dc, sl st in first ch sp, ch 3, 2 dc in same sp, fasten off.

Row 129: For **second point,** with wrong side of row 128 facing you, join with sl st in next shell, beg shell, ch 3, skip next ch-3 sp, (sc in next ch-3 sp, ch 3) 5 times, skip next ch-3 sp, shell in next shell leaving remaining sts unworked, turn.

Rows 130-137: Repeat same rows of first point. For **remaining five points,** repeat rows 129-137 of 2nd point. ✎

Homespun Country

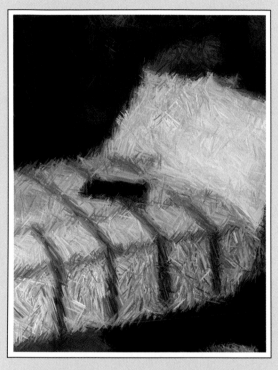

Rustic stripes and hearty plaids are a celebration of the informal warmth and unassuming charm of classic American country. Comforting, familiar, and as decorative as they are practical, these afghans are right at home in rooms filled with pottery, time-worn woods and family heirlooms.

Field of Ruffles

by designer Diane Simpson

Enticingly lush and warm, this richly-hued afghan will be a welcomed comfort on cool fall evenings. It's easy to make with its crocheted base and rows of colorful rippling ruffles.

Finished Size

58" x 81".

Materials

Worsted-weight yarn — 23 oz. each off-white, lt. peach, med. peach, dk. peach and rust; tapestry needle; I crochet hook or size needed to obtain gauge.

Gauge

5 dc sts = 2"; 3 dc rows = 2".

Skill Level

★ Easy

Instructions

Afghan

Row 1: With lt. peach, ch 147, sc in 2nd ch from hook, sc in each ch across, turn (146).

Row 2: Working this row in **front lps** *(see fig. 1, page 154)*, ch 3, dc in each st across, turn.

Row 3: Working this row in **back lps,** ch 3, dc in each st across, turn.

Rows 4-5: Repeat rows 2 and 3. Fasten off at end of last row.

Row 6: Working this row in **front lps,** join med. peach with sl st in first st, ch 3, dc in each st across, turn.

Rows 7-9: Repeat rows 3 and 2 alternately, ending with row 3. Fasten off at end of last row.

Rows 10-121: Repeat rows 6-9 consecutively, working in color sequence of dk. peach, rust, off-white, lt. peach and med. peach, ending with off-white. **Do not** fasten off at end of last row.

Row 122: Working this row in **front lps,** ch 1, sc in each st across, fasten off.

Ruffles

With right side of row 1 facing you, working in **front lps,** join lt. peach with sc in first st, sc in next st, *(hdc, 2 dc) in next st, (2 dc, hdc) in next st, sc in each of next 2 sts; repeat from * across, fasten off.

Matching colors, repeat ruffles in **front lps/back lps** of rows 2-122. ∞

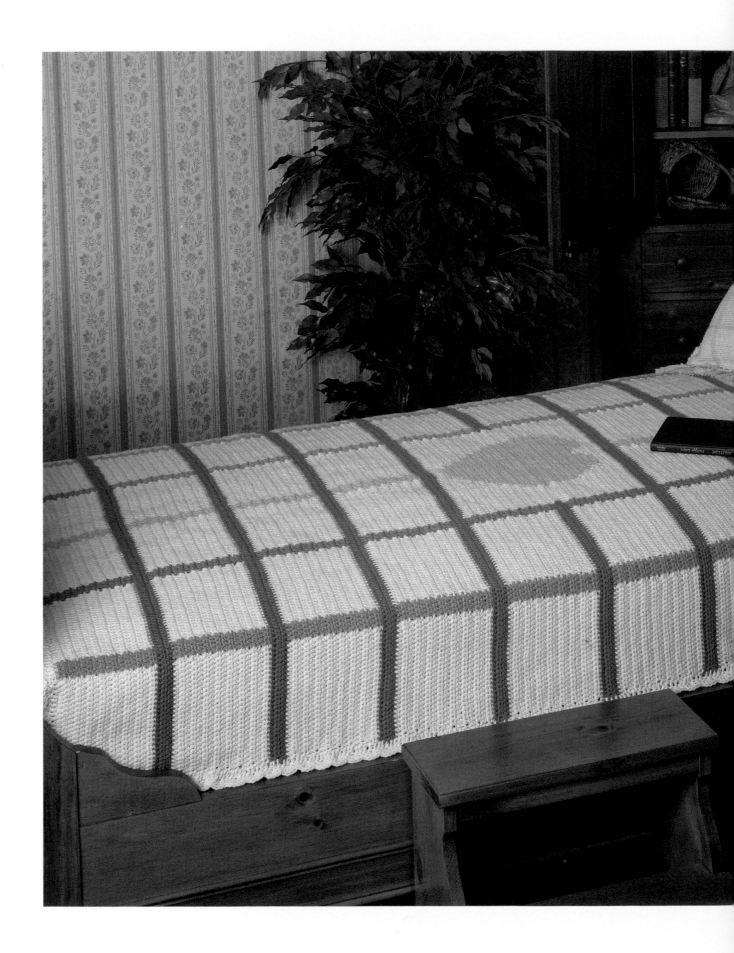

Cozy Plaid

by designer Barbara Nowicki

Created in soft country colors, this afghan is cozy enough to warm the chilliest winter nights. Whether it's used as a bedspread or just for snuggling, this handsome throw will warm your heart.

Finished Size

54" x 72".

Materials

100% cotton 4-ply yarn — 28 oz. off-white, 5 oz. each yellow and brown, 3 oz. each pink, green, blue and plum; tapestry needle; G crochet hook or size needed to obtain gauge.

Gauge

7 hdc sts = 2"; 3 hdc rows = 1".

Skill Level

★★ Average

Instructions

Afghan

Note: When changing colors *(see fig. 12, page 156),* always drop all colors to same side of work. **Do not** carry dropped colors across to next section of same color. Use a separate ball of yarn for each color section. Fasten off at end of each color section.

Row 1: With off-white, ch 177, hdc in 3rd ch from hook, hdc in next 24 chs, hdc in each ch across changing colors in the following sequence: 4 plum, 26 off-white, 4 blue, 26 off-white, 4 yellow, 26 off-white, 4 green, 26 off-white, 4 pink, 26 off-white, turn (176).

Rows 2-16: Working in established color pattern, ch 2, hdc in each st across, turn. Fasten off all colors at end of last row.

Row 17: Join brown with sl st in first st, ch 2, hdc in each st across, turn.

Rows 18-19: Ch 2, hdc in each st across, turn. **Do not** turn at end of last row, fasten off.

Row 20: Join off-white with sl st in first st, ch 2, hdc in each st across changing colors according to established color pattern on row 16, turn.

Rows 21-76: Repeat rows 2-20 consecutively, ending with row 19.

Rows 77-111: Ch 2, hdc in next 59 sts continuing established color pattern; follow graph below for next 56 sts; continue established color pattern on last 60 sts, turn.

Rows 112-115: Repeat rows 17-20.

Rows 116-187: Repeat rows 2-20 consecutively, ending with row 16. **Do not** fasten off off-white at end of last row.

Border

Notes: For **beginning shell (beg shell),** (ch 3, dc, ch 2, 2 dc) in first st.

For **shell** *(see fig. 22, page 157),* (2 dc, ch 2, 2 dc) in next st.

Rnd 1: Working around outer edge, beg shell, dc in each st and in end of each row around with shell in each corner, join with sl st in top of ch-3.

Rnd 2: Ch 1, sc in first st, skip next st, shell in next ch-2 sp, skip next st, (sc in next st, skip next st, shell in next st/ch-2 sp, skip next st) around, join with sl st in first sc, fasten off.∽

GRAPH

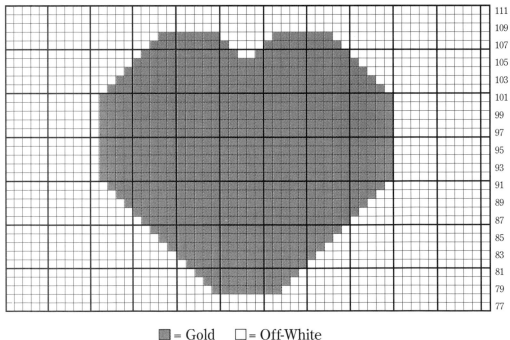

☐ = Gold   ☐ = Off-White

Quilted Stencils

by designer Kathleen Bernier Williford

Capture the down-home look of American country stencils. Use two easy block patterns in several combinations of six country colors, then set together with a wide, quilt-look border.

Quilted Stencils

Finished Size

49" x 68" without fringe.

Materials

Worsted-weight yarn — 25 oz. cream, 11 oz. dk. blue, 9 oz. lt. blue, 7 oz. green, 4 oz. each gold and burgundy; tapestry needle; I crochet hook or size needed to obtain gauge.

Gauge

3 sc sts = 1"; 3 sc rows = 1".

Skill Level

★★ Average

Instructions

Square A (make 18)

Notes: When changing colors *(see fig. 12, page 156),* always drop all colors to same side of work. **Do not** carry dropped colors across to next section of same color. Use a separate ball of yarn for each color section. Fasten off colors when no longer needed.

Use separate skein of cream for each section.

Wind lt. blue into four balls of 2 oz. each; wind green into four balls of 1½ oz. each; wind burgundy and gold into four balls of 1 oz. each.

Make squares in color combinations shown on Assembly Diagram on next page.

Row 1: With dk. blue, ch 27, sc in 2nd ch from hook, sc in next ch changing to green, sc in next 22 chs changing to dk. blue in last st made, sc in each of last 2 chs, turn (26).

Rows 2-26: Ch 1, sc in each st across changing colors according to Graph A on next page, turn. **Do not** fasten off dk. blue at end of last row.

Rnd 27: Working around outer edge, ch 1, sc in each st and in end of each row around with 3 sc in each corner, join with sl st in first sc, fasten off.

Square B (make 17)

Work same as Square A, changing colors according to Graph B on next page.

To **join,** with tapestry needle and dk. blue, sew squares together according to Assembly Diagram.

For **border,** working around entire outer edge of afghan, join dk. blue with sc in any st, sc in each st around with 3 sc in each corner, join with sl st in first sc, fasten off.

Fringe

For **each fringe,** cut two strands each 10" long. With both strands held together, fold in half, insert hook in st, draw fold through st, draw all loose ends through fold, tighten. Trim ends.

Fringe in every stitch on each short end of afghan using colors shown on Assembly Diagram. ∞

ASSEMBLY DIAGRAM

GRAPH A

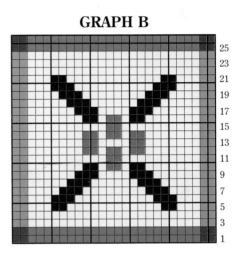

25
23
21
19
17
15
13
11
9
7
5
3
1

GRAPH B

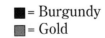

25
23
21
19
17
15
13
11
9
7
5
3
1

☐ = Cream   ▦ = Green   ■ = Burgundy
▦ = Dk. Blue   ▦ = Lt. Blue   ▦ = Gold

Aran Cables

by designer Vida Sunderman

Capture the feel of an Irish fisherman sweater in this timeless afghan. A joy to create with its variety of stitches, this stylish accent will add sophistication to your decor.

Finished Size

43½" x 57" without fringe.

Materials

Worsted-weight yarn — 43 oz. off-white; tapestry needle; J crochet hook or size needed to obtain gauge.

Gauge

3 dc sts = 1"; 3 dc rows = 2".

Skill Level

★★ Average

Instructions

Afghan

Row 1: Ch 169, dc in 4th ch from hook, dc in each ch across, turn (167).

Row 2: Ch 1, sc in each st across, turn.

Row 3: Ch 1, sc in first st; for **front post (fp)** *(see fig. 23, page 158),* insert hook around post of next st, complete as sc; fp around each st across with sc in last st, turn (165 fp, 2 sc).

Row 4: Ch 3, dc in each st across, turn (167 dc).

Row 5: Ch 1, sc in each st across, turn.

Row 6: Ch 3; for **diagonal st, skip next st, dc in each of next 2 sts; working in front of sts just made, yo, insert hook from back to front in skipped st, draw up 1" long lp, (yo, draw through 2 lps on hook) 2 times;** diagonal st across with dc in last st, turn (55 diagonal sts, 2 dc).

Rows 7-11: Repeat rows 5 and 6 alternately, ending with row 5.

Rows 12-13: Repeat rows 4 and 5.

Row 14: Ch 1, sc in first st; for **back post (bp),** insert hook around post of next st, complete as sc; bp around each st across with sc in last st, turn (165 bp, 2 sc).

Row 15: Ch 3, dc in each st across, turn.

Note: You may want to practice working this stitch with scrap yarn to insure ease of tension.

Row 16: Ch 2; for **weave st, yo, insert hook in next st, yo, draw lp through st and first lp on hook, yo, draw through 2 lps on hook, yo, insert hook in same st, yo, draw through both lps on hook;** (skip next st, weave st in next st) across with hdc in last st, turn (83 weave sts, 2 hdc).

Note: Maintain the stitch count of 83 weave sts.

Rows 17-30: Ch 2, weave st in each space between weave sts across with weave st over last ch-2 sp, turn.

Row 31: Ch 3, dc in each st across, turn (167).

Rows 32-105: Repeat rows 2-31 consecutively, ending with row 15.

Rnd 106: Working around outer edge, ch 1, sc in each st, in each corner and in end of each row around with 2 sc in end of each dc row and diagonal st row, join with sl st in first sc, fasten off.

Fringe

For **each fringe,** cut three strands each 12" long. With all three strands held together, fold in half, insert hook in st, draw fold through st, draw all loose ends through fold, tighten. Trim ends.

Fringe in every stitch on short ends of afghan.

Autumn Fields

by designer Eleanor Albano

The browns and golds of autumn are pleasingly highlighted by touches of vivid purple in this luxuriously thick, soft afghan. The easy hexagonal blocks make this a great carry-along project.

Finished Size

44" x 62".

Materials

Worsted-weight yarn — 17 oz. each med. brown and dk. gold, 13 oz. reddish-brown, 8 oz. each lt. gold and purple; tapestry needle; J crochet hook or size needed to obtain gauge.

Gauge

Rnd 1 = 2" across.

Skill Level

★★ Average

Instructions

Motif (make 72)

Notes: For **beginning cluster (beg cl),** ch 2, (yo, insert hook in same sp, yo, draw lp through, yo, draw through 2 lps on hook) 2 times, yo, draw through all 3 lps on hook.

For **cluster (cl)** *(see fig. 27, page 158),* (yo, insert hook in sp, yo, draw lp through, yo, draw through 2 lps on hook) 3 times in same sp, yo, draw through all 4 lps on hook.

For **beginning cluster shell (beg cl shell),** (beg cl, ch 3, cl) in same sp.

For **cluster shell (cl shell),** (cl, ch 3, cl) in next ch sp.

Rnd 1: With purple, ch 8, sl st in first ch to form ring, beg cl in ring, ch 3, (cl in ring, ch 3) 5 times, join with sl st in top of beg cl, fasten off (6 cls, 6 ch sps).

Rnd 2: Join lt. gold with sl st in any ch sp, beg cl shell, ch 2, (cl shell, ch 2) around, join, fasten off (6 cl shells, 6 ch sps).

Rnd 3: Join dk. gold with sl st in ch-3 sp of any cl shell, beg cl shell, ch 2, cl in next ch-2 sp, ch 2, *cl shell in ch-3 sp of next shell, ch 2, cl in next ch-2 sp, ch 2; repeat from * around, join, fasten off (12 ch-2 sps, 6 cl shells, 6 cls).

Rnd 4: Join med. brown with sl st in ch-3 sp of any cl shell, ch 3, (2 dc, ch 2, 3 dc) in same sp, 3 dc in each of next 2 ch-2 sps, *(3 dc, ch 2, 3 dc) in ch-3 sp of next cl shell, 3 dc in each of next 2 ch-2 sps; repeat from * around, join with sl st in top of ch-3, fasten off (72 dc, 6 ch-2 sps).

Rnd 5: Join reddish-brown with sc in any corner ch-2 sp, sc in same sp, sc in each st around with 2 sc in each ch-2 sp, join with sl st in first sc, fasten off.

Using reddish-brown, working in **back lps** *(see fig. 1, page 154),* sl st motifs together according to diagram below. ∞

ASSEMBLY DIAGRAM

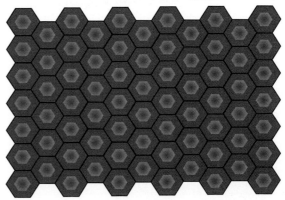

Spice Plaid

by designer Aline Suplinskas

Reminiscent of herbs and spices, the warm tones in this plaid afghan will add a homey touch to your favorite room.

Finished Size

49" x 55".

Materials

Worsted-weight yarn — 38 oz. dk. rust, 10 oz. each brown/beige/green multicolor and lt. green, 8 oz. dk. green, 7 oz. lt. rust; tapestry needle; G crochet hook or size needed to obtain gauge.

Gauge

4 hdc sts = 1"; 5 hdc rows = 2".

Skill Level

★★ Average

Instructions

Afghan

Notes: Row 1 is **wrong** side of work.

Ch-2 at beginning of each row counts as first st.

Row 1: With dk. rust, ch 195, hdc in 3rd ch from hook, hdc in next 10 chs, (ch 1, skip next ch, hdc in next 12 chs) across, turn (180 hdc, 14 ch sps).

Rows 2-9: Ch 2, hdc in next 11 hdc, (ch 1, skip next ch sp, hdc in next 12 hdc) across, turn.

Row 10: Ch 1, sc in first hdc, *ch 2, skip next 2 hdc, sc in next hdc, (ch 1, skip next hdc, sc in next hdc) 4 times*, [ch 1, skip next ch sp, sc in next hdc; repeat between **]; repeat between [ ] across, turn, fasten off (90 sc, 89 ch sps).

Row 11: Join multicolor with sl st in first sc, ch 2, hdc in same st, 2 hdc in each of next 5 sc, *ch 1, skip next ch sp, 2 hdc in each of next 6 sc; repeat from * across, turn (180 hdc, 14 ch sps).

Rows 12-15: Repeat row 2.

Row 16: Repeat row 10.

Row 17: With dk. rust, repeat row 11.

Rows 18-26: Repeat rows 2-10.

Rows 27-137: Repeat rows 11-26 consecutively, working in color sequence of lt. green, dk. rust, lt. rust, rust, multicolor and dk. rust, ending with row 25 and dk. rust. Fasten off at end of last row.

Vertical Stripes

With right side of afghan facing you, join dk. green with sl st in foundation ch below first column of ch sps, (ch 2, sl st in next ch sp) across length of afghan, fasten off. Repeat in each column of ch sps across, ending with 14 Vertical Stripes.

Horizontal Stripes

With right side of afghan facing you, join dk. green with sl st around post of first sc on row 10, (ch 1, sl st around post of next sc) across, fasten off. Repeat across each repeat of row 10, ending with 16 Horizontal Stripes.

For **edging,** working around entire outer edge of afghan, with right side of afghan facing you, join dk. green with sc in first hdc of row 137, ch 1, sc in same st, *ch 1, skip next hdc or ch sp, (sc in next hdc or ch sp, ch 1, skip next hdc or ch sp) across to next corner, (sc, ch 1, sc) in corner, ch 1, (sl st in end of next row, ch 1) across to next corner*, (sc, ch 1, sc) in cor-

ner; repeat between ** one more time, join with sl st in first sc, fasten off.

Fringe

For **each fringe,** cut one strand each dk. rust, lt. green, dk. green and multicolor each 11" long. With all four strands held together, fold in half, insert hook in sp, draw fold through sp, draw all loose ends through fold, tighten. Trim ends.

Fringe in each ch sp across short ends of afghan.∽

Rustic Stripes

by designer Aline Suplinskas

Choose a few favorite colors to make this boldly-striped afghan, or get out your scrap bag and make each stripe a different color. Either way, you'll have a wonderful treasure.

Finished Size

51" x 69".

Materials

Worsted-weight yarn — 14 oz. each of seven assorted colors; tapestry needle; K crochet hook or size needed to obtain gauge.

Gauge

1 dc st = 3"; 1 dc **back lp** row = 1¼".

Skill Level

★ Easy

Instructions

Afghan

Notes: Work entire pattern in **back lps** *(see fig. 1, page 154).*

Use 2 strands same-color yarn held together throughout.

Ch-3 counts as first st of each row.

Row 1: With first color, ch 158, dc in 6th ch from hook, dc in same ch, 2 dc in next ch, skip next 2 chs, (2 dc in each of next 2 chs, skip next 2 chs) across with dc in last ch, turn (154 dc).

Row 2: Ch 3, skip next st, 2 dc in each of next 2 sts, (skip next 2 sts, 2 dc in each of next 2 sts) across to last 2 sts, skip next st, dc in last st, turn, fasten off.

Row 3: Join next color with sl st in first st, repeat row 2, **do not** fasten off.

Rows 4-86: Repeat rows 2 and 3 alternately, working in desired color pattern and ending with row 2.∽

*R*ich Textures

*Nubby bobbles and popcorns,
curving cables and ruffles – these are
the appealing accents that make an
afghan a delight to see and touch.
Showcase your favorite yarn with the
dimensional texture of interesting
raised crochet stitches, and
create an afghan that's sure to
please, year after year.*

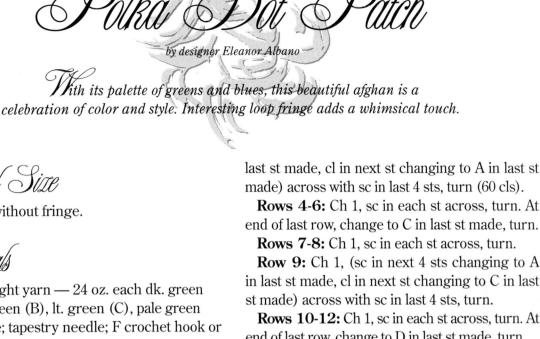

Polka Dot Patch

by designer Eleanor Albano

With its palette of greens and blues, this beautiful afghan is a celebration of color and style. Interesting loop fringe adds a whimsical touch.

Finished Size

62" x 65½" without fringe.

Materials

Worsted-weight yarn — 24 oz. each dk. green (A), med. green (B), lt. green (C), pale green (D) and blue; tapestry needle; F crochet hook or size needed to obtain gauge.

Gauge

5 sc sts = 1"; 9 sc rows = 2".

Skill Level

★★ Average

Instructions

Afghan

Notes: For **cluster (cl)** *(see fig. 27, page 158)*, *yo, insert hook in st, yo, draw lp through, yo, draw through 2 lps on hook; repeat from * 2 more times in same st, yo, draw through all 4 lps on hook, ch 1.

Wrong side of cl is right side of work.

When changing colors *(see fig. 12, page 156)*, work over dropped color. Fasten off at end of each color section.

Row 1: With A, ch 305, sc in 2nd ch from hook, sc in each ch across, turn (304).

Row 2: Ch 1, sc in each st across, turn.

Row 3: Ch 1, (sc in next 4 sts changing to B in last st made, cl in next st changing to A in last st made) across with sc in last 4 sts, turn (60 cls).

Rows 4-6: Ch 1, sc in each st across, turn. At end of last row, change to C in last st made, turn.

Rows 7-8: Ch 1, sc in each st across, turn.

Row 9: Ch 1, (sc in next 4 sts changing to A in last st made, cl in next st changing to C in last st made) across with sc in last 4 sts, turn.

Rows 10-12: Ch 1, sc in each st across, turn. At end of last row, change to D in last st made, turn.

Rows 13-14: Ch 1, sc in each st across, turn.

Row 15: Ch 1, (sc in next 4 sts changing to C in last st made, cl in next st changing to D in last st made) across with sc in last 4 sts, turn.

Rows 16-18: Ch 1, sc in each st across, turn. At end of last row, change to B in last st made, turn.

Rows 19-20: Ch 1, sc in each st across, turn.

Row 21: Ch 1, (sc in next 4 sts changing to D in last st made, cl in next st changing to B in last st made) across with sc in last 4 sts, turn (60 cls).

Rows 22-24: Ch 1, sc in each st across, turn. At end of last row, change to A in last st made, turn.

Rows 25-26: Ch 1, sc in each st across, turn.

Rows 27-288: Repeat rows 3-26 consecutively, ending with row 24. At end of last row, **do not** change colors, fasten off.

For **trim**, working around posts of stitches on row 6, join blue with sc in first st, sc in each st across, fasten off. Repeat in every 6th row of afghan.

Edging

Row 1: Working in ends of rows, join blue with sc in first row, sc in each row across, turn (288).

Row 2: Ch 1, sc in first st, (ch 20, sc in next st) across, fasten off.

Repeat on opposite side of afghan. ∽

Lovely Lace

by designer Dorris Brooks

You'll be ready to herald the arrival of spring with this tasseled beauty.

Finished Size

46" x 75½ " not including tassels.

Materials

Worsted-weight yarn — 46 oz. lilac; tapestry needle; I crochet hook or size needed to obtain gauge.

Gauge

3 dc sts = 1"; 8 shell rows = 5".

Skill Level

★★ Average

Instructions

Afghan

Note: For **shell** *(see fig. 22, page 157)*, (2 dc, ch 2, 2 dc) in next ch or ch-2 sp.

Row 1: Ch 155, dc in 4th ch from hook, skip next 2 chs, shell in next ch, skip next 2 chs, *dc in next 8 chs, skip next ch, (dc, ch 1, dc) in next ch, skip next ch, dc in next 8 chs, skip next 2 chs, shell in next ch, skip next 2 chs; repeat from * 5 more times, dc in each of last 2 chs, turn (112 dc, 7 shells, 6 ch-1 sps).

Note: For **back post stitch (bp)** *(see fig. 23, page 158)*, yo, insert hook from back to front around post of st on previous row, complete as dc.

Row 2: Ch 3, bp around next st, shell in next shell, bp around next st, *dc in next 6 sts, skip next st, bp around next st, (dc, ch 1, dc) in next ch-1 sp, bp around next st, skip next st, dc in next 6 sts, bp around next st, shell in next shell, bp in next st; repeat from * 5 more times, dc in last st, turn (86 dc, 26 bp, 7 shells, 6 ch-1 sps).

Row 3: Ch 3, fp around next bp, shell in next shell, fp around next bp, *dc in next 5 sts, skip next st, fp around next bp, (2 dc, ch 1, 2 dc) in next ch-1 sp, fp around next bp, skip next st, dc in next 5 sts, fp around next bp, shell in next shell, fp around next bp; repeat from * 5 more times, dc in last st, turn (86 dc, 26 fp, 7 shells, 6 ch-1 sps).

Row 4: Ch 3, bp around next fp, shell in next shell, bp around next fp, *dc in next 4 sts, skip next st, bp around next fp, (3 dc, ch 1, 3 dc) in next ch-1 sp, bp around next fp, skip next st, dc in next 4 sts, bp around next fp, shell in next shell, bp around next fp; repeat from * 5 more times, dc in last st, turn.

Row 5: Ch 3, fp around next bp, shell in next shell, fp around next bp, *dc in each of next 3 sts, skip next st, fp around next bp, (4 dc, ch 1, 4 dc) in next ch-1 sp, fp around next bp, skip next st, dc in each of next 3 sts, fp around next bp, shell in next shell, fp around next bp; repeat from * 5 more times, dc in last st, turn.

Row 6: Ch 3, bp around next fp, shell in next shell, bp around next fp, *dc in next 7 sts, skip next st, (dc, ch 1, dc) in next ch-1 sp, skip next st, dc in next 7 sts, bp around next fp, shell in next shell, bp around next fp; repeat from * 5 more times, dc in last st, turn (98 dc, 14 bp, 7 shells, 6 ch-1 sps).

Rows 7-11: Working in fp instead of bp and bp instead of fp, repeat rows 2-6.

Rows 12-121: Repeat rows 2-11 consecutively.

Row 122: Ch 1, sc in each st across with 2

continued on page 64

Clusters & Ruffles

by designer Barbara Nowicki

Rows and rows of generous ruffles and cushiony clusters make this afghan a snuggly soft comfort. Make it in warm country colors or choose your own favorites.

Finished Size

55" x 72".

Materials

Worsted-weight yarn — 30 oz. off-white, 12 oz. each dusty rose, teal, gold and brown; tapestry needle; H crochet hook or size needed to obtain gauge.

Gauge

7 sc sts = 2"; 7 sc rows = 2".

Skill Level

★★ Average

Instructions

Afghan

Notes: For **cluster (cl)** *(see fig. 27, page 158),* (yo, insert hook in st, yo, draw lp through, yo, draw through 2 lps on hook) 4 times in next st, yo, draw through all 5 lps on hook.

The treble crochet used in row 2 gives a raised effect.

Row 1: With dusty rose, ch 252, sc in 2nd ch from hook, sc in each ch across, turn (251).

Notes: Push all tr and cls through to right side when working.

Row 1 is right side of work.

Row 2: Ch 1, sc in first st, (tr in next st, sc in next st) across, turn (126 sc, 125 tr).

Row 3: Ch 1, sc in each st across, turn.

Rows 4-6: Repeat rows 2 and 3 alternately, ending with row 2.

Rows 7-9: Ch 1, sc in each st across, turn.

Row 10: Ch 1, sc in first st, cl in next st, (sc in each of next 3 sts, cl in next st) across with sc in last st, turn (188 sc, 63 cls).

Row 11: Ch 1, sc in each st across, turn (251).

Row 12: Ch 1, sc in each of first 3 sts, (cl in next st, sc in each of next 3 sts) across, turn.

Row 13: Ch 1, sc in each st across, turn.

Row 14: Repeat row 10.

Rows 15-17: Ch 1, sc in each st across, turn.

Row 18: Repeat row 2.

Row 19: Ch 1, sc in each st across, turn.

Rows 20-23: Repeat rows 4-7. Fasten off at end of last row.

Row 24: With wrong side of last row facing you, working this row in **back lps** *(see fig. 1, page 154),* join off-white with sc in first st, (ch 5, sc in next st) across, turn.

Row 25: Working in **front lps** on row before last, sc in each st across, turn.

Rows 26-29: Repeat rows 24 and 25 alternately. Fasten off at end of last row.

Row 30: Join teal with sc in first st, (tr in next st, sc in next st) across, turn.

Rows 31-191: Repeat rows 3-30 consecutively, working in color sequence of gold, brown, gold, teal and dusty rose, ending with row 23. ∽

Blue Diamonds

by designer Evelyn Coate

Raised diamond patterns cascade down this warm, comfortable afghan. Make it in easy care acrylic yarn for washability, and use it all year long in the den or family room.

Finished Size

47" square.

Materials

Sport yarn — 46 oz. blue; tapestry needle; H crochet hook or size needed to obtain gauge.

Gauge

7 sc sts = 2"; 7 sc **back lp** *(see fig. 1, page 154),* rows = 2".

Skill Level

★★ Average

Instructions

Afghan

Notes: For **fringe**, leave 3" strand yarn at beginning and end of each row. **Do not** turn at the end of a row.

All sc are worked in **back lps.**

For **raised double crochet (rdc),** dc in **front lp** of next st on row before last, skip next st on the row you are working.

Row 1: Ch 165, **do not** turn, fasten off. Join with sc in first ch, sc in each ch across, fasten off (165).

Rows 2-3: Working in **back lps,** join with sc in first st, sc in each st across, fasten off.

Row 4: Join with sc in first st, sc in next 9 sts, rdc in next st, (sc in next 15 sts, rdc in next st) 9 times, sc in last 10 sts, fasten off (155 sc, 10 rdc).

Row 5: Join with sc in first st, sc in next 8 sts, rdc in next st, sc in next st, rdc in next st, (sc in next 13 sts, rdc in next st, sc in next st, rdc in next st) 9 times, sc in last 9 sts, fasten off (145 sc, 20 rdc).

Row 6: Join with sc in first st, sc in next 7 sts, *rdc in next st, (sc in next st, rdc in next st) 2 times*, [sc in next 11 sts; repeat between **]; repeat between [ ] 8 more times, sc in last 8 sts, fasten off (135 sc, 30 rdc).

Row 7: Join with sc in first st, sc in next 6 sts, *rdc in next st, (sc in next st, rdc in next st) 3 times*, [sc in next 9 sts; repeat between **]; repeat between [ ] 8 more times, sc in last 7 sts, fasten off (125 sc, 40 rdc).

Row 8: Join with sc in first st, sc in next 5 sts, *rdc in next st, (sc in next st, rdc in next st) 4 times*, [sc in next 7 sts; repeat between **]; repeat between [ ] 8 more times, sc in last 6 sts, fasten off (115 sc, 50 rdc).

Row 9: Join with sc in first st, sc in next 4 sts, *rdc in next st, (sc in next st, rdc in next st) 5 times*, [sc in next 5 sts; repeat between **]; repeat between [ ] 8 more times, sc in last 5 sts, fasten off (105 sc, 60 rdc).

Row 10: Join with sc in first st, sc in each of next 3 sts, *rdc in next st, (sc in next st, rdc in next st) 6 times*, [sc in each of next 3 sts; repeat between **]; repeat between [ ] 8 more times, sc in last 4 sts, fasten off (95 sc, 70 rdc).

Row 11: Join with sc in first st, sc in each of next 2 sts, rdc in next st, (sc in next st, rdc in next st) across to last 3 sts, sc in each of last 3 sts, fasten off (85 sc, 80 rdc).

Row 12: Join with sc in first st, (sc in next st, rdc in next st) across with sc in each of last 2 sts, fasten off (84 sc, 81 rdc).

Row 13: Repeat row 11.

Row 14: Join with sc in first st, sc in each of next 3 sts, rdc in next st, (sc in next st, rdc in next st) 6 times, [sc in each of next 3 sts, rdc in next st, (sc in next st, rdc in next st) 6 times]; repeat between [ ] 8 more times, sc in last 4 sts, fasten off (95 sc, 70 rdc).

Row 15: Join with sc in first st, sc in next 4 sts, rdc in next st, (sc in next st, rdc in next st) 5 times, [sc in next 5 sts, rdc in next st, (sc in next st, rdc in next st) 5 times]; repeat between [ ] 8 more times, sc in last 5 sts, fasten off (105 sc, 60 rdc).

Row 16: Join with sc in first st, sc in next 5 sts, rdc in next st, (sc in next st, rdc in next st) 4 times, [sc in next 7 sts, rdc in next st, (sc in next st, rdc in next st) 4 times]; repeat between [ ] 8 more times, sc in last 6 sts, fasten off (115 sc, 50 rdc).

Row 17: Join with sc in first st, sc in next 6 sts, rdc in next st, (sc in next st, rdc in next st) 3 times, [sc in next 9 sts, rdc in next st, (sc in next st, rdc in next st) 3 times]; repeat between [ ] 8 more times, sc in last 7 sts, fasten off (125 sc, 40 rdc).

Row 18: Join with sc in first st, sc in next 7 sts, rdc in next st, (sc in next st, rdc in next st) 2 times, [sc in next 11 sts, rdc in next st, (sc in next st, rdc in next st) 2 times]; repeat between [ ] 8 more times, sc in last 8 sts, fasten off (135 sc, 30 rdc).

Row 19: Join with sc in first st, sc in next 8 sts, rdc in next st, sc in next st, rdc in next st, (sc in next 13 sts, rdc in next st, sc in next st, rdc in next st) 9 times, sc in last 9 sts, fasten off (145 sc, 20 rdc).

Rows 20-164: Repeat rows 4-19 consecutively, ending with row 4.

Row 165: Working in **back lps,** join with sl st in first st, sl st in each st across, fasten off.∝⊸

Lovely Lace continued from page 59

sc in each ch-2 sp and one sc in each ch-1 sp, fasten off.

Tassel

For **each tassel,** cut 15 strands each 14" long. Tie separate strand tightly around middle of all strands. Wrap 20" strand 1" from top of fold, secure. Trim ends.

Tie tassel to center of each point across each short end of afghan. ∝⊸

Popcorn Hearts

by designer Carol Smith

*This lighthearted afghan is made with just twelve big, beautiful blocks.
It adds a bit of loveable peach charm to a living room or bedroom.*

Popcorn Hearts

Finished Size

Block is 15½" across. Afghan is 49½" x 65".

Materials

Worsted-weight yarn — 63 oz. peach; tapestry needle; J crochet hook or size needed to obtain gauge.

Gauge

10 dc sts = 3"; 7 dc rows = 4".

Skill Level

★★ Average

Instructions

Block (make 12)

Rnd 1: Ch 4, sl st in first ch to form ring, ch 5, (2 dc, ch 2) 3 times in ring, dc in ring, join with sl st in 3rd ch of ch-5 (8 dc, 4 ch sps).

Notes: For **beginning popcorn (beg pc),** ch 3, 3 dc in same st, remove lp from hook, insert hook in top of ch-3, draw lp through, ch 1.

For **popcorn (pc)** *(see fig. 24, page 158),* 4 dc in next st, remove lp from hook, insert hook in first st, draw lp through, ch 1.

When working into pc, work into ch-1 instead of top of pc.

For **shell** *(see fig. 22, page 157),* (2 dc, ch 2, 2 dc) in next ch sp.

Rnd 2: Beg pc, shell, (pc in each of next 2 sts, shell) around with pc in last st, join with sl st in top of beg pc (8 pc, 4 shells).

Rnds 3-4: Beg pc, dc in each dc, shell in each ch sp and pc in each pc around, join, ending with 8 pc, 4 shells and 32 dc.

Rnd 5: Beg pc, *dc in next 5 sts, pc in next st, shell, pc in next st, dc in next 5 sts*, [pc in each of next 2 pc; repeat between **]; repeat between [ ] around with pc in last pc, join (16 pc, 4 shells, 40 dc).

Rnds 6-7: Repeat rnd 3, ending with 16 pc, 4 shells and 72 dc.

Rnd 8: Beg pc, *(dc in next 5 sts, pc in next pc) 2 times, shell, (pc in next st, dc in next 5 sts) 2 times*, [pc in each of next 2 pc; repeat between **]; repeat between [ ] around with pc in last pc, join (24 pc, 4 shells, 80 dc).

Rnd 9: Beg pc, *dc in next 5 sts, pc in next pc, dc in next 4 sts, pc in next st, dc in each of next 3 sts, shell, dc in each of next 3 sts, pc in next st, dc in next 4 sts, pc in next pc, dc in next 5 sts*, [pc in each of next 2 pc; repeat between **]; repeat between [ ] around with pc in last pc, join (24 pc, 4 shells, 96 dc).

Rnd 10: Beg pc, *dc in next 7 sts, pc in each of next 2 sts, dc in next 7 sts, shell, dc in next 7 sts, pc in each of next 2 sts, dc in next 7 sts*, [pc in each of next 2 pc; repeat between **]; repeat between [ ] around with pc in last pc, join (24 pc, 4 shells, 112 dc).

Rnd 11: Beg pc, *dc in next 18 sts, shell, dc in next 18 sts*, [pc in each of next 2 pc; repeat between **]; repeat between [ ] around with pc in last pc, join (8 pc, 4 shells, 144 dc).

Rnd 12: Repeat rnd 3 (8 pc, 4 shells, 160 dc).

Rnd 13: Beg pc, *dc in each of next 2 sts, (pc in each of next 2 sts, dc in each of next 2 sts) around to next ch sp, (pc, ch 2, pc) in next ch sp*; repeat between ** 3 more times, dc in each of next 2 sts, (pc in each of next 2 sts, dc in each of next 2 sts) around with pc in last pc, join, fasten off (96 pc, 4 ch sps, 96 dc).

Matching sts and ch sps, sew Blocks together in three rows with four Blocks in each.

Edging

Rnd 1: Join with sl st in first corner ch sp on short end of afghan, (ch 3, dc, ch 2, 2 dc) in same ch sp, *dc in next 48 sts, (dc in each of next 2 ch sps, dc in next 48 sts) around to next corner ch sp*, [shell; repeat between **]; repeat between [ ] around, join with sl st in top of ch-3 (4 shells, 708 dc).

Rnd 2: Ch 3, dc in each dc and shell in each ch sp around, join (4 shells, 720 dc).

Rnd 3: Beg pc, dc in next st, pc in next st, dc in next st, *(pc, dc, pc) in next ch sp, (dc in next st, pc in next st) around to next ch sp, (dc, pc, dc) in next ch sp*, (pc in next st, dc in next st) around to next ch sp; repeat between ** one more time, (pc in next st, dc in next st) around, join with sl st in top of beg pc, fasten off. ∞

Windsor Cables

by designer Vicki Watkins

This classically-styled throw, elegant in off-white and navy, makes the ideal gift for the man in your life. Its textured panels blend beautifully with traditional decor.

Finished Size

43" x 53" not including fringe.

Materials

Worsted-weight yarn — 33½ oz. blue and 27½ oz. white; tapestry needle; H crochet hook or size needed to obtain gauge.

Gauge

7 hdc sts = 2"; rows 1-9 = 3".

Skill Level

★★ Average

Instructions

Afghan

Row 1: With blue, ch 187, hdc in 3rd ch from hook, hdc in each ch across, turn (186 hdc).

Note: For **half double crochet back post (hdc bp)** *(see fig. 23, page 158),* yo, insert hook from back to front around post of st on previous row, complete as hdc.

Row 2: Ch 2, hdc bp around each st across with hdc in last st, turn.

Row 3: Ch 2, hdc in each st across, turn.

Note: For **double crochet front post (dc fp)** *(see fig. 23, page 158),* yo, insert hook from front to back around post of st on previous row, complete as dc.

Row 4: Ch 2, hdc in next st, (dc fp around each of next 2 sts, hdc in each of next 2 sts) across, turn.

Row 5: Ch 2, hdc in each st across, turn.

Note: For **treble crochet front post (tr fp)** *(see fig. 23, page 158),* yo 2 times, insert hook from front to back around post of st on row before last, complete as tr.

Row 6: Ch 2, hdc in next st, *skip next 2 sts, skip next 2 dc fp on row before last, tr fp around each of next 2 dc fp, skip next 2 sts on last row; working behind tr fp, hdc in each of next 2 sts; working in front of last 2 tr fp, tr fp around each of first 2 skipped dc fp, skip next 2 sts on last row, hdc in each of next 2 sts; repeat from * across, turn.

Row 7: Ch 2, hdc in each st across, turn.

Rows 8-9: Repeat rows 2 and 3. Fasten off at end of last row.

Row 10: Join white with sc in first st, sc in each st across, turn.

Rows 11-13: Repeat rows 3 and 2 alternately, ending with row 3.

Rows 14-19: Repeat rows 4-9.

Rows 20-29: With blue, repeat rows 10-19.

Rows 30-129: Repeat rows 10-29 consecutively.

Fringe

For **each fringe,** cut four strands each 10" long. With all four strands held together, fold in half, insert hook in end of row, draw fold through, draw all loose ends through fold, tighten. Trim ends.

With white, work four fringe evenly spaced in end of each white stripe and with blue, work four fringe evenly spaced in end of each blue stripe.

Repeat on other end of afghan. ∽

Classic Ripples

A gentle rhythm of increasing and
decreasing produces an afghan that
is a classic crochet favorite. Lengthwise
ripples create a soothing wave pattern,
and tassels and popcorns add lively
interest. A reversible ripple is perfect
for even the chilliest winter evening.

Tasseled Points

by designer Diane Simpson

*Country elegance at its finest!
Interesting texture is provided by easy
shell stitches, while tassels add refinement
to this easy-care, versatile afghan.*

Finished Size

40" x 61" without tassels.

Materials

Worsted-weight yarn — 46 oz. burgundy;
tapestry needle; I crochet hook or size needed to
obtain gauge.

Gauge

6 pattern rows = 5".

Skill Level

★ Easy

Instructions

Afghan

Notes: For **shell** *(see fig. 22, page 157)*, (2 dc, ch
1, 2 dc) in next ch or st.

For **point,** (3 dc, ch 1, 3 dc) in next ch or st.
Afghan may ruffle slightly until blocked.

Row 1: Ch 249, dc in 6th ch from hook, *(skip
next 2 chs, shell in next ch, skip next 2 chs, dc in
next ch) 2 times, skip next 2 chs, point in next
ch, skip next 2 chs, dc in next ch; repeat
between ( ) 2 times*, [skip next 4 chs, dc in next
ch; repeat between **]; repeat between [ ] 5
times, skip next 2 chs, dc in last ch, turn (28

shells, 7 points, 44 dc).

Row 2: Ch 3, skip next dc, *(dc in next shell, shell in next dc) 2 times, skip next 2 dc of next point, dc in next dc, shell in next ch-1 sp, dc in next dc, skip next 2 dc of same point, (shell in next dc, dc in next shell) 2 times*, [skip next 6 dc; repeat between **]; repeat between [ ] 5 times, skip next dc, dc in top of ch-5, turn.

Rows 3-71: Ch 3, skip next dc, *(dc in next shell, shell in next dc) 2 times, skip next dc of next shell, dc in next dc, shell in next ch-1 sp, dc in next dc, skip next dc of same shell, (shell in next dc, dc in next shell) 2 times*, [skip next 6 dc; repeat between **]; repeat between [ ] 5 times, skip next dc, dc in top of ch-3, turn. Fasten off at end of last row.

Tassel

For **each tassel,** cut 42 strands each 16" long. Tie separate strand tightly around middle of all strands. Wrap 30" strand 1½" from top of tassel, secure. Trim ends.

Tie tassel to center of each point across short ends of afghan.∝⌐

Fascination Ripple

by designer Sandra Smith

Thick and cushy waves reverse for a surprising effect in this extra-thick afghan. It's fascinating to watch this pattern take shape, row after row.

Fascination Ripple

Finished Size

57" x 58".

Materials

Worsted-weight yarn — 72 oz. green, 9 oz. variegated, 5 oz. each lt. green, apricot, white and coral; tapestry needle; J crochet hook or size needed to obtain gauge.

Gauge

5 sc sts = 2"; 3 sc rows = 1".

Skill Level

★★ Average

Instructions

Afghan

Note: For **single crochet decrease (sc dec),** draw up lp in next st/ch, skip next st/ch, draw up lp in next st/ch, yo, draw through all 3 lps on hook.

Row 1: With green, ch 184, sc in 2nd ch from hook, sc in next 5 chs, sc dec, *sc in next 5 chs, (sc, ch 2, sc) in next ch, sc in next 5 chs, sc dec; repeat from * 11 times, sc in last 6 chs, turn (169 sc, 12 ch-2 sps).

Row 2: Ch 1, 2 sc in first st, sc in next 4 sts, sc dec, *sc in next 5 sts, (sc, ch 2, sc) in next ch sp, sc in next 5 sts, sc dec; repeat from * 11 times, sc in next 4 sts, 2 sc in last st, turn.

Note: For **double crochet decrease (dc dec),** yo, insert hook in next st, yo, draw lp through, yo, draw through 2 lps on hook, yo, skip next st, insert hook in next st, yo, draw lp through, yo, draw through 2 lps on hook, yo, draw through all 3 lps on hook.

Row 3: Ch 3, dc in same st, dc in next 4 sts, dc dec, *dc in next 5 sts, (dc, ch 2, dc) in next ch sp, dc in next 5 sts, dc dec; repeat from * 11 times, dc in next 4 sts, 2 dc in last st, turn.

Rows 4-5: Repeat row 2. Fasten off at end of last row and **do not** turn.

Notes: For **treble front post (tr fp)** *(see fig. 23, page 158),* yo 2 times, insert hook from right to left around post of st on row indicated, complete as tr.

For **treble front post decrease (tr fp dec),** *yo 2 times, insert hook from front to back around post of next st on row indicated, yo, draw lp through, (yo, draw through 2 lps on hook) 2 times*, skip next st/tr fp dec; repeat between **, yo, draw through all 3 lps on hook.

Row 6: Working all sc on last row and in each st across, and all tr fp on last dc row made, join green with sc in first sc, tr fp around first dc, sc in same sc as last sc made, tr fp around same dc, (sc in next sc, tr fp around next dc) 4 times, sc in next sc, tr fp dec, skip next sc dec, *sc in next sc, (tr fp around next dc, sc in next sc) 5 times, tr fp around same dc as last fp, (sc, ch 2, sc) in next ch sp, tr fp around next dc, sc in next sc, tr fp around same dc, sc in next sc, (tr fp around next dc, sc in next sc) 4 times, tr fp dec, skip next sc dec; repeat from * 11 times, sc in next sc, (tr fp around next dc, sc in next sc) 4 times, tr fp around last dc, sc in last sc, tr fp around same dc, sc in same sc, **do not** turn, fasten off (169 sc, 157 tr fp).

Row 7: Join variegated with sc in first st, skip next tr fp, (sc in next sc, skip next tr fp) 5 times, sc dec, *(skip next tr fp, sc in next sc) 5 times, skip next tr fp and next sc, (sc, ch 2, sc) in next ch sp, skip next sc and next tr fp, (sc in next sc, skip next tr fp) 5 times, sc dec; repeat from * 11 times, (skip next tr fp, sc in next sc) 6 times, turn

(169 sc, 12 ch sps).

Row 8: Repeat row 2, fasten off.

Row 9: Working all sc on last row and all tr fp around tr fp 2 rows before last, join green with sc in first sc, tr fp around first tr fp, sc in same sc, tr fp around same fp as last fp, (sc in next sc, tr fp around next tr fp) 4 times, sc in next sc, tr fp dec, skip next sc dec, *sc in next sc, (tr fp around next tr fp, sc in next sc) 5 times, tr fp around same fp as last fp, (sc, ch 2, sc) in next ch sp, tr fp around next tr fp, sc in next sc, tr fp around same fp as last fp, sc in next sc, (tr fp around next tr fp, sc in next sc) 4 times, tr fp dec, skip next sc dec; repeat from * 11 times, sc in next sc, (tr fp around next tr fp, sc in next sc) 4 times, tr fp around last tr fp, sc in last sc, tr fp around same tr fp, sc in same sc, **do not** turn, fasten off.

Rows 10-11: With coral, repeat rows 7 and 8.

Row 12: Repeat row 9.

Rows 13-14: With white, repeat rows 7 and 8.

Row 15: Repeat row 9.

Rows 16-17: With apricot, repeat rows 7 and 8.

Row 18: Repeat row 9.

Rows 19-20: With lt. green, repeat rows 7 and 8.

Row 21: Repeat row 9.

Rows 22-23: Repeat rows 7 and 8.

Row 24: Repeat row 9, **turn, do not** fasten off.

Row 25: Ch 1, sc in first st, skip next tr fp, (sc in next sc, skip next tr fp) 5 times, sc dec, *(skip next tr fp, sc in next sc) 5 times, skip next tr fp and next sc, (sc, ch 2, sc) in next ch sp, skip next sc and next tr fp, (sc in next sc, skip next tr fp) 5 times, sc dec; repeat from * 11 times, (skip next tr fp, sc in next sc) 6 times, turn.

Row 26: Repeat row 2, fasten off.

Row 27: Repeat row 9.

Rows 28-172: Repeat rows 7-27 consecutively, ending with row 25.

Rows 173-174: Repeat row 2. Fasten off at end of last row.✑

Rippled Wheat

by designer Eleanor Albano

What could be more inviting on a chilly evening than a comfortable chair and a cozy afghan? It's reversible, and abundantly textured in fuzzy, worsted-weight yarn.

Finished Size

39" x 62" not including tassels.

Materials

Fuzzy worsted-weight yarn — 65 oz. beige; tapestry needle; J crochet hook or size needed to obtain gauge.

Gauge

7 dc sts = 2"; 4 dc rows = 3".

Skill Level

★ Easy

Instructions

Afghan

Notes: For **dc back post (dc bp)** *(see fig. 23, page 158),* yo, insert hook from back to front around post of next st, complete as dc.

For **dc front post (dc fp)** *(see fig. 23, page 158),* yo, insert from front to back around post of next st, complete as dc.

(Ch 3, dc next 2 sts tog) at beginning of each row counts as first dc.

For **dc next 5 chs/sts tog,** *yo, insert hook in next ch/st, yo, draw 1p through, yo, draw through 2 lps on hook; repeat from * 4 times, yo, draw through all 6 lps on hook.

Row 1: Ch 195, dc 4th and 5th chs from hook tog, dc in next 5 chs, (2 dc, ch 1, 2 dc) in next ch, dc in next 5 chs, [dc next 5 chs tog, dc in next 5 chs, (2 dc, ch 1, 2 dc) in next ch, dc in next 5 chs]; repeat between [ ] across to last 3 chs, dc last 3 chs tog, turn (181 dc, 12 ch sps).

Row 2: Ch 3, dc bp next 2 sts tog, dc fp in next 5 sts, (2 dc, ch 1, 2 dc) in next ch sp, dc fp in next 5 sts, [dc bp next 5 sts tog, dc fp in next 5 sts, (2 dc, ch 1, 2 dc) in next ch sp, dc fp in next 5 sts]; repeat between [ ] across to last 3 sts, dc bp next 2 sts tog leaving ch-3 unworked, turn.

Row 3: Ch 3, dc fp next 2 sts tog, *dc bp in next 5 sts, (2 dc, ch 1, 2 dc) in next ch sp, dc bp in next 5 sts*, [dc fp next 5 sts tog; repeat between **]; repeat between [ ] across to last 3 sts, dc fp next 2 sts tog leaving ch-3 unworked, turn.

Rows 4-85: Repeat rows 2 and 3 alternately. Fasten off at end of last row.

Tassel (make 25)

Cut 25 strands yarn each 7" long. Tie separate strand yarn tightly around middle of all strands, fold all 25 strands in half. Wrap 16" strand yarn 1" from top of tassel, secure. Trim ends.

Tie tassel to each point on short ends of afghan.

Tropical Waves

by designer Eleanor Albano

Dream of warm sea breezes as you relax beneath these waves of tropical color. Get away for rest and relaxation with this bright throw, even if it's just to the sunporch.

Finished Size

41" x 53½" not including fringe.

Materials

Worsted-weight yarn — 8½ oz. each jade (B), teal (C), turquoise (D), lt. blue (E), blue (F), periwinkle (G) and lilac (H), 4 oz. each emerald (A) and dk. iris (I); tapestry needle; J crochet hook or size needed to obtain gauge.

Gauge

3 sc sts = 1"; 11 pattern rows = 4".

Skill Level

★ Easy

Instructions

Afghan

Note: For **puff st** *(see fig. 26, page 158),* yo, insert hook in next st, yo, draw lp through, yo, insert hook in same st, yo, draw lp through, yo, draw through all 5 lps on hook.

Row 1: With A, ch 161, sc in 2nd ch from hook, sc in each of next 3 chs, puff st in next 4 chs, (sc in next 4 chs, puff st in next 4 chs) across, turn, fasten off (80 sc, 80 puff sts).

Row 2: Join B with sc in first st, sc in each of next 3 sts, puff st in next 4 sts, (sc in next 4 sts, puff st in next 4 sts) across, turn, fasten off.

Rows 3-113: Working in color sequence of C, D, E, F, G, H, I, H, G, F, E, D, C, B, A and B, repeat row 2, ending with A in last row.

Edging

Row 1: Join A with sc in end of row 1, sc in end of each row across, turn.

Row 2: Ch 1, sc in each st across, turn, fasten off.

Repeat on other side.

Fringe

For **each fringe,** cut two 8" strands of each color. With all strands held together, fold in half, insert hook in st, draw fold through, draw all loose ends through fold, tighten. Trim ends.

Fringe in each st on edging, matching color sequence.❧

Shifting Sands

by designer Eleanor Albano

Popcorn stitches in a gentle pattern create a soothing, soft afghan. In subtle, neutral tones, it's the perfect handmade accent for a contemporary or traditional room.

Finished Size

45½" x 58".

Materials

Fuzzy worsted-weight yarn — 25 oz. beige, 18 oz. off-white and 11 oz. white; tapestry needle; J crochet hook or size needed to obtain gauge.

Gauge

10 sts = 3"; 7 pattern rows = 4".

Skill Level

★★ Average

Instructions

Afghan

Notes: To **dc next 3 chs/sts tog** *(see fig. 18, page 157),* (yo, insert hook in next ch/st, yo, draw lp through, yo, draw through 2 lps on hook) 3 times, yo, draw through all 4 lps on hook.

Tr sts worked in row 2 create the popcorn look.

Row 1: With beige, ch 154, dc in 4th ch from hook, *dc in each of next 3 chs, dc next 3 chs tog, dc in each of next 3 chs*, [3 dc in next ch; repeat between **]; repeat between [ ] across with 2 dc in last ch, turn (151).

Row 2: Ch 1, 2 sc in first st, *tr in next st, sc in next st, tr in next st, sc next 3 sts tog, tr in next st, sc in next st, tr in next st*, [(sc, tr, sc) in next st; repeat between **]; repeat between [ ] across with 2 sc in last st, turn.

Row 3: Ch 3, dc in same st, *dc in each of next 3 sts, dc next 3 sts tog, dc in each of next 3 sts*, [3 dc in next st; repeat between **]; repeat between [ ] across with 2 dc in last st, turn.

Rows 4-6: Repeat rows 2 and 3 alternately, ending with row 2. Fasten off at end of last row.

Row 7: Join off-white with sl st in first st, ch 3, dc in same st, *dc in each of next 3 sts, dc next 3 sts tog, dc in each of next 3 sts*, [3 dc in next st; repeat between **]; repeat between [ ] across with 2 dc in last st, turn.

Rows 8-10: Repeat rows 2 and 3 alternately, ending with row 2. Fasten off at end of last row.

Row 11: With white, repeat row 7.

Row 12: Repeat row 2, fasten off.

Row 13: With beige, repeat row 7.

Rows 14-101: Repeat rows 2-13 consecutively, ending with row 5. Fasten off at end of last row.

Rippling Shells

by designer Sandra Smith

Liven up a country room with cool, crisp shells of blue and white. Made with an unexpected combination of shell stitches and ripples, this throw will become a family favorite.

Finished Size

36½" x 52".

Materials

Worsted-weight yarn — 14½ oz. blue, 12 oz. lt. blue and 7 oz. white; tapestry needle; J crochet hook or size needed to obtain gauge.

Gauge

1 shell = 2½", 3 sc sts = 1"; 3 sc **back lp** rows = 1".

Skill Level

★ Easy

Instructions

Afghan

Notes: For **shell,** (4 tr, ch 2, 4 tr) in next st or ch.

For **V-stitch (V-st),** (sc in next ch, ch 2, sc in next ch).

For **decrease (dec),** (insert hook in next st, yo, draw lp through), skip next st; repeat between ( ), yo, draw through all 3 lps on hook.

Row 1: With blue, ch 154, sl st in 2nd ch from hook, (skip next 3 chs, shell in next ch, skip next 3 chs, sl st in next ch) across, **do not** turn, fasten off (20 sl sts, 19 shells).

Row 2: Working the following rows in **back lps** *(see fig. 1, page 154),* join lt. blue with sc in first sl st, skip next st, sc in each of next 3 sts, V-st, sc in each of next 3 sts, (dec, sc in each of next 3 sts, V-st, sc in each of next 3 sts) across to last 2 sts, skip next st, sc in last sl st, turn (134 sc, 19 V-sts).

Rows 3-7: Ch 1, sc in first st, skip next st, sc in each of next 3 sts, V-st, sc in each of next 3 sts, (dec, sc in each of next 3 sts, V-st, sc in each of next 3 sts) across to last 2 sts, skip next st, sc in last st, turn. Fasten off at end of last row

Row 8: Working this row in **both lps,** join white with sl st in first st, ch 4, 3 tr in same st, skip next 4 sts, sl st in next ch-2 sp, skip next 4 sts, (shell in next st, skip next 4 sts, sl st in next ch-2 sp, skip next 4 sts) across with 4 tr in last st, **do not** turn, fasten off (19 sl sts, 18 shells, 8 tr).

Row 9: Working the following rows in **back lps,** join blue with sc in first st, sc in same st, sc in each of next 2 sts, dec, (sc in each of next 3 sts, V-st, sc in each of next 3 sts, dec) across to last 3 sts, sc in each of next 2 sts, 2 sc in last st, turn (135 sc, 18 V-sts).

Rows 10-14: Ch 1, 2 sc in first st, sc in each of next 2 sts, dec, (sc in each of next 3 sts, V-st, sc in each of next 3 sts, dec) across to last 3 sts, sc in each of next 2 sts, 2 sc in last st, turn. Fasten off at end of last row.

Row 15: Working this row in **both lps,** join lt. blue with sl st in first st, skip next 3 sts, shell in next st, skip next 3 sts, (sl st in next ch-2 sp, skip next 3 sts, shell in next st, skip next 3 sts) across with sl st in last st, turn, fasten off.

Rows 16-21: With white, repeat rows 2-7.
Row 22: With blue, repeat row 8.
Rows 23-28: With lt. blue, repeat rows 9-14.
Row 29: With white, repeat row 15.

continued on page 102

Filet Ripple

by designer Darla J. Fanton

Refreshing, cool mint is the color of choice for this breeze of an afghan. It's made with soft, 100% cotton yarn for a muted look that will prepare your decor for warmer weather.

Finished Size

50" x 71".

Materials

100% cotton 4-ply yarn — 54 oz. green; tapestry needle; G crochet hook or size needed to obtain gauge.

Gauge

4 dc sts = 1"; 2 dc rows = 1".

Skill Level

★★ Average

Instructions

Afghan

Notes: For **mesh,** ch 2, skip next 2 chs or dc, dc in next ch or dc.

For **block,** dc in each of next 2 chs or dc, dc in next ch or dc.

For **beginning block (beg block),** ch 3, dc in each of next 2 chs or dc, dc in next ch or dc.

For **ending increase (end inc)** *(see ill. below right),* *yo, insert hook in same st as last dc made, yo, draw lp through, yo, draw through one lp on hook, (yo, draw through 2 lps on hook) 2 times, working in lp indicated on illustration; repeat from * 2 times.

For **beginning increase (beg inc),** ch 5, dc in 4th ch from hook, dc in next ch, dc in next dc.

Row 1: Ch 288, dc in 4th ch from hook, dc in each of next 2 chs (first block made), complete row according to graph below, turn.

Rows 2-101: Working according to graph, repeat rows 2-11 on graph consecutively. Fasten off at end of last row.

ENDING INCREASE ILLUSTRATION

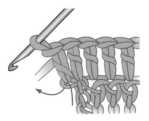

□ = Mesh

▨ = Block

■ = Ch 1, sl st in first 4 sts

⊠ = Beg Block

▼ = End Inc

▽ = Beg Inc

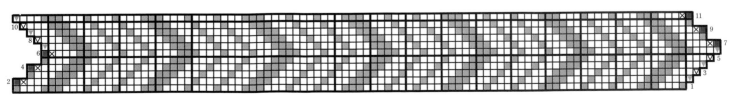

Popcorn & Ripples

by designer Diane Simpson

Lovely warm colors and big popcorn stitches create a smashing combination in this out-of-the-ordinary afghan. There is sure to be a perfect spot in your home for this heirloom throw.

Finished Size

44" x 56" without tassels.

Materials

Worsted-weight yarn — 12 oz. each off-white (A), lt. peach (B), med. peach (C), dk. peach (D) and rust (E); tapestry needle; I crochet hook or size needed to obtain gauge.

Gauge

3 dc sts = 1"; 5 dc rows = 3".

Skill Level

★★ Average

Instructions

Afghan

Note: To **dc next 5 chs/sts tog,** *yo, insert hook in next ch/st, yo, draw lp through, yo, draw through 2 lps on hook; repeat from * 4 times, yo, draw through all 6 lps on hook.

Row 1: With A, ch 188, 2 dc in 4th ch from hook, (dc in next 5 chs, dc next 5 chs tog, dc in next 5 chs), *5 dc in next ch, dc in next 10 chs, dc next 5 chs tog, dc in next 10 chs, 5 dc in next ch; repeat between ( ); repeat from * across with 3 dc in last ch, turn (185).

Row 2: Ch 3, 2 dc in same st, (dc in next 5 sts, dc next 5 sts tog, dc in next 5 sts), *5 dc in next st, dc in next 10 sts, dc next 5 sts tog, dc in next 10 sts, 5 dc in next st; repeat between ( ); repeat from * across with 3 dc in last st, turn, fasten off.

Note: For **popcorn (pc)** *(see fig. 24, page 158),* 5 dc in next st, drop lp from hook, insert hook in first st of 5-dc group, pick up dropped lp, draw through st. Push to right side of work.

Row 3: Join B with sl st in first st, ch 3, 2 dc in same st, dc in next 5 sts, *skip next st, pc, skip next 3 sts*, dc in next 5 sts, [(pc, ch 1, pc, ch 1, pc) in next st, dc in next 10 sts; repeat between **, dc in next 10 sts, (pc, ch 1, pc, ch 1, pc) in next st, dc in next 5 sts; repeat between ** one more time, dc in next 5 sts]; repeat between [ ] across with 3 dc in last st, turn, fasten off (136 dc, 33 pc).

Row 4: Join C with sl st in first st, ch 3, 2 dc in same st, *dc in next 5 sts, dc next 5 sts tog, dc in next 5 sts/ch-1 sps*, [5 dc in next st, dc in next 10 sts, dc next 5 sts tog, dc in next 10 sts/ch-1 sps, 5 dc in next st; repeat between **]; repeat between [ ] across with 3 dc in last st, turn, fasten off (185).

Rows 5-66: Repeat rows 3 and 4 alternately, working in color sequence of one row each of D, E, A, B and C, ending with A. **Do not** fasten off at end of last row.

Row 67: Repeat row 2.

Tassel (make 19)

For **each tassel,** cut 20 strands E each 13" long. Tie separate strand tightly around middle of all strands. Wrap 30" strand ¾" from top of tassel, secure. Trim ends.

Tie tassel to each point on short ends of afghan. ∞

Just for Baby

*Welcome the new baby with a soft,
cozy afghan. Sweet dreams come
easily under a downy-soft cover
created in subtle colors and pretty yarns
selected especially for the little one.*

Little Boy Blue

by designer Frances Hughes

It's the perfect gift for the new little boy in your life — a soft, baby blue blanket with cuddly cluster stitches and interesting crocheted cross stitches.

Finished Size

34" x 43".

Materials

3-ply sport yarn — 15 oz. lt. blue; tapestry needle; No. 0 steel crochet hook or size needed to obtain gauge.

Gauge

4 sc sts = 1"; 9 sc rows = 2".

Skill Level

★★ Average

Instructions

Afghan

Row 1: Ch 121, sc in 2nd ch from hook, sc in each ch across, turn (120 sc).

Row 2: Ch 1, sc in each st across, turn.

Row 3: Ch 1, sc in each st across, **do not** turn, fasten off.

Note: For **front cross stitch (fcr)** *(see fig. 20, page 157),* skip next st, dc in next st; working in front of dc just made, dc in skipped st.

Row 4: Join with sl st in first st, ch 3, fcr across with dc in last st, **do not** turn, fasten off (59 fcr, 2 dc).

Row 5: Join with sc in top of ch-3, sc in each st across, **do not** turn, fasten off (120).

Rows 6-8: Repeat rows 4 and 5 alternately, ending with row 4.

Row 9: Join with sc in first st, sc in each st across, turn.

Rows 10-11: Repeat rows 2 and 3.

Row 12: Join with sl st in first st, ch 2, hdc in each st across, turn.

Row 13: Ch 3, dc in each st across, turn.

Note: For **cluster (cl)** *(see fig. 27, page 158),* *yo, insert hook in next st, yo, draw lp through, yo, draw through 2 lps on hook; repeat from * 2 times in same st, yo, draw through all 4 lps on hook.

Row 14: Ch 4, skip next st, cl in next st, (ch 1, skip next st, cl in next st) across with dc in last st, turn (59 cls, 59 ch-1 sps, 2 dc).

Row 15: Ch 3, dc in each st and in each ch across, turn (120).

Row 16: Ch 2, hdc in each st across, **do not** turn, fasten off.

Row 17: Repeat row 9.

Rows 18-123: Repeat rows 2-17 consecutively, ending with row 11.

Edging

Rnd 1: Join with sc in first st, sc in each st across with 3 sc in last st; working in ends of rows, evenly space 140 sc across, 3 sc in corner st, sc in each st across with 3 sc in last st; working in ends of rows, evenly space 140 across, 2 sc in same st as first st, join with sl st in first sc, **turn** (528).

Rnd 2: Ch 2, hdc in each st around with 3 hdc in each corner st, join with sl st in top of ch-2, **do not** turn (536).

continued on page 102

Ducks on Parade

by designer Lou Ann Millsaps

Soft yellow ducklings adorn every other block on this checkerboard afghan — the remaining blocks are easy solid-color single crochet. Add polish with pretty satin bows.

Finished Size

35" x 51".

Materials

3-ply sport yarn — 18 oz. yellow, 11 oz. lavender and small amount orange; 4 yds. purple ¼" satin picot ribbon; tapestry needle; F and G crochet hooks or sizes needed to obtain gauges.

Gauge

F hook, 9 sc sts = 2"; 9 sc rows = 2". G hook, 4 sc sts = 1"; 4 sc rows = 1".

Skill Level

★★ Average

Instructions

Solid Square (make 7)

Row 1: Using G hook and yellow, ch 45, sc in 2nd ch from hook, sc in each ch across, turn (44).

Rows 2-38: Ch 1, sc in each st across, turn. At end of last row, **do not** turn.

Rnd 39: Working around outer edge, with F hook, ch 1, sc in end of each row and in each st around with 3 sc in each corner, join with sl st in first sc, fasten off.

Duck Square (make 8)

Notes: Cut number of yards required for each color section as indicated in graph on page 103; wind separate ball for each section. Cut one-yard lengths for small sections without numbers.

When changing colors *(see fig. 13, page 156)*, always drop all colors to same side of work. **Do not** carry dropped colors across to next section of same color. Use a separate ball or skein of yarn for each color section. Fasten off colors when no longer needed.

Row 1: Using G hook and lavender, ch 45, sc in 2nd ch from hook, sc in each ch across, turn (44).

Rows 2-38: Ch 1, sc in each st across changing colors according to graph on page 103, turn. At end of last row, change to yellow in last st, **do not** turn.

Rnd 39: Repeat same rnd of Solid Square.

Alternating Duck Squares with Solid Squares, sew together in three rows of five squares each.

Edging

Rnd 1: With right side of afghan facing you, using F hook and lavender, join with sc in any corner, sc in each st around with 3 sc in each corner, join with sl st in first sc.

Rnd 2: Sl st in each st around, join with sl st in first sl st, fasten off.

Tie ribbon into bow around each duck's neck.∞

graph on page 103

Vintage Lace

by designer Carol Smith

Made with a new twist on an old technique, this delicate baby afghan is lovely in yellow or ecru. Its lace is made using a 1" wide ruler, and it's finished with a pretty scalloped border.

Finished Size

51" x 52".

Materials

3-ply baby pompadour yarn — 34 oz. yellow; 1" wide plastic or wooden ruler without cutting edge; tapestry needle; F crochet hook or size needed to obtain gauge.

Gauge

4 sc sts = 1"; 4 sc rows = 1".

Skill Level

★★ Average

Instructions

Afghan

Row 1: Ch 201, sc in 2nd ch from hook, sc in each ch across, turn (200).

Notes: For **crossed stitch (cr st)** *(see fig. 19, page 157),* skip next st, dc in next st; working over dc just made, dc in skipped st.

For **hdc lattice loop,** working over ruler (see diagram below), yo, insert hook in next st, yo, draw lp through and up to top of ruler, yo, draw through all 3 lps on hook, ch 1.

For **double treble crochet (dtr)** *(see fig. 8, page 155),* yo 3 times, insert hook in st, yo, draw through, (yo, draw through 2 lps on hook) 4 times.

For **ruler substitute,** use a sturdy 1" x 6"

strip of cardboard.

Row 2: Ch 3, cr st across with dc in last st, turn (99 cr sts, 2 dc).

Row 3: Ch 1, sc in each st across, turn (200).

Row 4: Ch 6, work hdc lattice loop in each st across, turn.

Row 5: Ch 1, sc in each st across skipping ch-1 sps, sc in top of ch-6, turn (200).

Rows 6-99: Repeat rows 2-5 consecutively, ending with row 3.

Rnd 100: For **border,** working around outer edge, in sts and in ends of rows, ch 5, 10 dtr in same st, skip next 2 sts, sc in next st, skip next 3 sts, (9 dtr in next st, skip next 3 sts, sc in next st, skip next 3 sts) 24 times, 11 dtr in next corner st, skip next cr st row, sc in next sc row, (skip next lattice row, 9 dtr in next sc row, skip next cr st row, sc in next sc row) 24 times, skip next 2 sts, 9 dtr in next st, skip next 3 sts, sc in next st, (skip next 3 sts, 9 dtr in next st, skip next 3 sts, sc in next st) 24 times, skip next cr st row, (9 dtr in next sc row, skip next lattice row, sc in next sc row, skip next cr st row) 24 times, join with sl st in top of ch-5, fasten off.

HDC LATTICE LOOP DIAGRAM

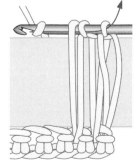

Pretty Baby

by designer Aline Suplinskas

An easy zigzag pattern makes this softly-striped shawl a wonderful beginner project. Choose acrylic baby yarn for easy-care washability.

Finished Size

29" x 34½" without fringe.

Materials

Baby pompadour yarn — 5½ oz. each green and white; tapestry needle; E crochet hook or size needed to obtain gauge.

Gauge

6 dc sts = 1"; 5 dc rows = 2".

Skill Level

★ Easy

Instructions

Afghan

Row 1: With green, ch 226, dc in 4th ch from hook, dc in next ch, skip next 3 chs, (sc in next ch, ch 3, dc in each of next 3 chs, skip next 3 chs) across with sc in last ch, turn (96 dc, 32 sc).

Row 2: Ch 3, 2 dc in first sc, (skip next 3 dc, sc in next ch, ch 3, dc in each of next 2 chs, dc in next sc) across to last 3 dc, skip next 2 dc, sc in top of ch-3, turn, fasten off.

Row 3: Join white with sl st in first st, ch 3, 2 dc in first sc, (skip next 3 dc, sc in next ch, ch 3, dc in each of next 2 chs, dc in next sc) across to last 3 dc, skip next 2 dc, sc in top of ch-3, turn.

Row 4: Ch 3, 2 dc in first sc, (skip next 3 dc, sc in next ch, ch 3, dc in each of next 2 chs, dc in next sc) across to last 3 dc, skip next 2 dc, sc in top of ch-3, turn, fasten off.

Rows 5-6: With green, repeat rows 3 and 2.

Rows 7-86: Repeat rows 3-6 consecutively.

Fringe

For **each fringe,** cut four green strands and three white strands each 8" long. With all seven strands held together, fold in half, insert hook in ch-3 sp, draw fold through, draw all loose ends through fold, tighten. Trim ends.

Fringe in each ch-3 sp at each short end of afghan.

Candy Stripes

by designer Kathy Wigington

Welcome the newest member of the family home in comfort with pastel stripes. Made with appealing crossed stitches, this afghan is easy and fun to crochet.

Finished Size

42" x 43".

Materials

Worsted-weight yarn — 12 oz. white, 4 oz. pink, 3 oz. each yellow, peach, green and blue; tapestry needle; H crochet hook or size needed to obtain gauge.

Gauge

7 dc sts = 2"; 2 dc rows = 1".

Skill Level

★ Easy

Instructions

Afghan

   Row 1: With pink, ch 142, dc in 4th ch from hook, dc in each ch across, turn (140).

   Row 2: Ch 3, dc in each st across, turn, fasten off.

   Notes: For **beginning cross stitch (beg cr st),** skip first st, join white with sl st in next st, ch 3, working over ch-3 just made, dc in skipped st.

   For **cross stitch (cr st)** *(see fig. 19, page 157),* skip next st, dc in next st, working over dc just made, dc in skipped st.

For uniformity, while making each cr st, draw up at least ¼" to ⅜" loop on hook.

Row 3: Beg cr st, cr st across, turn, fasten off (70 cr sts).

Row 4: Join blue with sl st in first st, ch 3, dc in each st across, turn.

Row 5: Ch 3, dc in each st across, **do not** turn, fasten off.

Rows 6-77: Repeat rows 3-5 working rows 4 and 5 in color sequence of green, peach, yellow, pink and blue, ending with pink.

Rnd 78: Working around outer edge, join white with sc in any corner, 2 sc in same sp, sc in each st and 2 sc in end of each row around with 3 sc in each corner, join with sl st in first sc.

Note: For **corner cross stitch (corner cr st),** dc in next st, working over dc just made, dc in same st as last cr st made.

Rnd 79: Sl st in next st, ch 3, working over ch-3 just made, dc in sl st, (corner cr st) 2 times, cr st around with 3 corner cr sts in each corner, join with sl st in top of ch-3.

Rnd 80: Ch 1, sc in each dc around with 3 sc in each corner, join with sl st in first sc, fasten off.∽

Little Boy Blue continued from page 93

Rnd 3: Ch 3, dc in each st around with 5 dc in each corner st, join with sl st in top of ch-3 (552).

Rnd 4: Ch 3, cl in same st, ch 1, *(skip next st, cl in next st, ch 1) across to 2 sts before next corner st, skip next 2 sts, (cl, ch 1) 2 times in next corner st; repeat from * 3 times, ch 1, skip next st, cl in next st, ch 1, skip last st, join with sl st in top of first cl (278 cls).

Rnd 5: Ch 1, sc in same st, ch 4, (sc in next cl, ch 4) around, join with sl st in first sc, **turn.**

Rnd 6: Sl st in next ch sp, ch 1, 3 sc in each ch sp around, join, fasten off.∽

Rippling Shells continued from page 85

Rows 30-35: With blue, repeat rows 2-7.

Row 36: Working on opposite side of starting ch, join blue with sl st in first st, (skip next 3 chs, shell in next ch, skip next 3 chs, sl st in next ch) across, **do not** turn, fasten off.

Rows 37-70: Repeat rows 2-35.∽

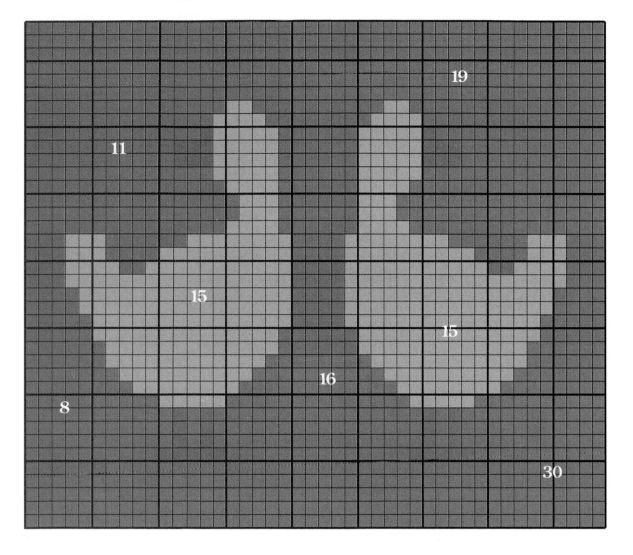

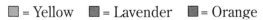

■ = Yellow   ■ = Lavender   ■ = Orange

One-Piece Favorites

*The possibilities of beginning with a
simple chain and adding one stitch
after another are wonderful! Stitch
by stitch, these afghans grow into
stunning creations that require
no sewing to complete.*

Zigzag Stripes

by designer Dorris Brooks

This lovely afghan is a crochet lover's delight! Even with its intricate-looking, reversible stitch pattern, it's easy to make.

Finished Size

45" x 66".

Materials

Worsted-weight yarn — 17 oz. each dk. pink, med. pink and lt. pink; tapestry needle; J crochet hook or size needed to obtain gauge.

Gauge

3 patt sts *(see note)* = 4"; 3 patt st rows = 2".

Note: For **pattern stitch (patt st),** skip next 3 chs or sts, tr in next ch or st; working as indicated around tr just made, dc in first skipped ch or st, dc in each of next 2 skipped chs or sts.

Skill Level

★ Easy

Instructions

Afghan

Row 1: With dk. pink, ch 202, dc in 4th ch from hook, (skip next 3 chs, tr in next ch; working **behind** tr just made, dc in first skipped ch, dc in each of next 2 skipped chs) across with dc in each of last 2 chs, turn (151 dc, 49 tr).

Row 2: Ch 3, dc in next dc, (skip next 3 dc, tr in next tr; working in **front** of tr just made, dc in first skipped dc, dc in each of next 2 skipped dc) across with dc in each of last 2 dc, turn, fasten off.

Row 3: Join med. pink with sl st in first st, ch 3, dc in next dc, (skip next 3 dc, tr in next tr; working **behind** tr just made, dc in first skipped dc, dc in each of next 2 skipped dc) across with dc in each of last 2 dc, turn.

Row 4: Repeat row 2, **do not** fasten off.

Row 5: Ch 3, dc in next dc, (skip next 3 dc, tr in next tr; working **behind** tr just made, dc in first skipped dc, dc in each of next 2 skipped dc) across with dc in each of last 2 dc, turn.

Row 6: Repeat row 2.

Row 7: With dk. pink, repeat row 3.

Row 8: Repeat row 2.

Rows 9-68: Repeat rows 3-8 consecutively, working in color sequence of 4 rows lt. pink, 2 rows dk. pink, 4 rows med. pink and 2 rows dk. pink.

Fringe

For **each fringe,** cut five strands yarn each 18" long. With all five strands held together, fold in half, insert hook in st, draw fold through st, draw all loose ends through fold, tighten. Trim ends.

Matching colors, fringe in end of each row on short ends of afghan.

Cozy Comfort

by designer Rosalie DeVries

The generous size of this colorful afghan makes it just right for a child to snuggle under for naps at home or in the car. For the wheelchair-bound, it's a snug and secure lap robe.

Finished Size

42" x 43".

Materials

Worsted-weight yarn — 9 oz. dk. aqua (D), 8 oz. med. aqua (E), 7 oz. each lt. aqua (F), dk. pink (B), lt. pink (C), 3½ oz. each maroon (A) and white (G); tapestry needle; G crochet hook or size needed to obtain gauge.

Gauge

4 dc sts = 1"; 2 dc rows = 1".

Skill Level

★ Easy

Instructions

Afghan

  Row 1: With A, ch 170, sc in 2nd ch from hook, sc in each ch across, turn, fasten off (169).

  Row 2: Join B with sl st in first st, sl st in next st, ch 3, dc in each of next 3 sts, ch 3, *sl st in next 3 sts, ch 3, dc in each of next 3 sts, ch 3; repeat from * across with sl st in last 2 sts, turn, fasten off (85 sl sts, 84 dc, 56 ch-3 sps).

  Row 3: Join C with sl st in first sl st, ch 3, *skip next sl st, sl st in top of next ch-3 sp, ch 3, dc in each of next 3 dc, ch 3, sl st in top of next ch-3 sp, skip next sl st, dc in next sl st; repeat from * across, turn, fasten off (112 dc, 57 ch-3 sps).

  Row 4: Join D with sl st in first dc, ch 3, *skip next sl st, sl st in top of next ch-3 sp, ch 3, dc in each of next 3 dc, ch 3, sl st in top of next ch-3 sp, skip next sl st*, [dc in next dc; repeat between **]; repeat between [ ] across with dc in top of last ch-3, turn, fasten off.

  Rows 5-84: Working in color sequence of E, F, G, F, E, D, C, B, A, B, C and D, repeat row 4, ending with B.

  Row 85: Join A with sl st in first dc, ch 4, hdc in top of next 5 ch-3 sps or in next dc, *tr in next dc, hdc in top of next 5 ch-3 sps or in next dc; repeat from * across with tr in top of last ch-3, **do not** turn, fasten (169).

  Rnd 86: Working around outer edge, join D with sl st in any corner, ch 2, 4 hdc in same sp, hdc in each st and 2 hdc in end of each row around with 5 hdc in each corner, join with sl st in top of ch-2, fasten off.

  Rnd 87: Join E with sc in any st, reverse sc *(see fig. 30, page 158)* in each st around, join with sl st in first sc, fasten off.

Island Breeze

by designer Dorris Brooks

Tropical colors of peach and pale blue bring to mind a restful vacation in a beautiful island paradise. Variegated yarn creates the interesting, multicolored cable effect.

Finished Size

47" x 70" not including fringe.

Materials

Worsted-weight yarn — 46 oz. peach (MC) and 17 oz. blue (CC); tapestry needle; J crochet hook or size needed to obtain gauge.

Gauge

20 dc sts = 7"; 8 dc rows = 5".

Skill Level

★★ Average

Instructions

Afghan

Row 1: With MC, ch 202, dc in 4th ch from hook, dc in each ch across, turn (200 dc).

Row 2: Ch 1, sc in each st across, turn, fasten off.

Notes: For **beginning cable (beg cable),** ch 3, skip next 2 sts, sc in next st, **turn,** sc in each of next 3 chs, sl st in next sc, **turn.**

For **cable,** ch 3, skip next 2 sts of last row, sc in next st, **turn,** sc in each of next 3 chs, sl st in next sc, **turn.**

Row 3: Join CC with sc in first st, beg cable; working behind cable, sc in each of next 2 skipped sts on last row, (cable; working behind cable, sc in each of next 2 skipped sts on last row) 65 times, turn, fasten off (66 cables).

Row 4: Join MC with sc in first st; working behind cables and skipping next 3 sts of cable, (sc in next st, 2 sc in next st, skip next sl st) 66 times, sc in last st, turn (200).

Row 5: Ch 3, dc in each st across, turn.

Row 6: Ch 3, dc in next st, (ch 1, skip next st, dc in each of next 2 sts) across, turn (66 ch-1 sps).

Row 7: Ch 3, dc in each st and in each ch sp across, turn.

Rows 8-11: Repeat rows 2-5.

Note: For **V-stitch (V-st)** *(see fig. 25, page 158x),* (dc, ch 1, dc) in next st.

Row 12: Ch 3, skip next st, V-st in next st, (skip next 2 sts, V-st in next st) 65 times, skip next st, dc in last st, turn (66 V-sts).

Rows 13-14: Ch 3, V-st in each ch-1 sp across with dc in last st, turn.

Row 15: Ch 3, dc in each st and in each ch sp across, turn.

Rows 16-95: Repeat rows 2-15 consecutively, ending with row 11. Fasten off at end of last row.

Fringe

For **each fringe,** cut three strands MC each 16" long. With all three strands held together, fold in half, insert hook in end of row, draw fold through row, draw all loose ends through fold, tighten. Trim ends.

Fringe in end of each dc row and in end of each cable row.

Calico Kitten

by designer Dorris Brooks

This airy, scalloped afghan is just right for early spring mornings on the porch. Its softly patterned, lushly fringed design is light as a cloud, yet warm as toast in fuzzy, sport-weight yarn.

Finished Size

43" x 63" without fringe.

Materials

Fuzzy novelty sport-weight yarn — 25 oz. multicolor; tapestry needle; I crochet hook or size needed to obtain gauge.

Gauge

1 patt st *(see notes below)* = 1¾"; 4 patt st rows = 3".

Skill Level

★ Easy

Instructions

Afghan

Notes: For **pattern stitch (patt st),** (4 dc, ch 2, dc) in next ch-2 sp.

For **V-stitch (V-st)** *(see fig. 25, page 158),* (dc, ch 1, dc) in next st.

Ch-3 at beginning of each row counts as first stitch.

Row 1: Ch 134, V-st in 4th ch from hook, skip next 2 chs, V-st in next ch, *skip next 3 chs, patt st in next ch, (skip next 4 chs, patt st in next ch) 2 times, skip next 3 chs, V-st in next ch, skip next 2 chs, V-st in next ch; repeat from * 5 times, dc in last ch, turn (18 patt sts, 14 V-sts, 2 dc).

Rows 2-84: Ch 3, V-st in ch-1 sp of each V-st and patt st in ch-2 sp of each patt st across with dc in top of ch-3, turn.

Row 85: Ch 3, V-st in each of next 2 V-sts, *(sc in next dc, skip next ch-2 sp, sc in next 4 dc) 3 times, V-st in each of next 2 V-sts; repeat from * across, dc in top of last ch-3, fasten off.

Fringe

For **each fringe,** cut four strands yarn each 16" long. With all four strands held together, fold in half, insert hook in st, draw fold through st, draw all loose ends through fold, tighten. Trim ends.

Fringe in every other stitch on short ends of afghan.∽

Rosebuds in Rows

by designer Shep Shepherd

Fuzzy, bulky-weight yarn in hues of cream, rose and green forms the basis of this soft and feminine throw. Green and cream panels are made first, then rosebuds and fringe are added.

Finished Size

45" x 52" without fringe.

Materials

Fuzzy bulky-weight yarn — 40 oz. cream, 11 oz. rose and 7 oz. dk. teal; tapestry needle; J crochet hook or size needed to obtain gauge.

Gauge

3 sc sts = 1"; 3 sc rows = 1".

Skill Level

★★ Average

Instructions

Afghan

Row 1: With cream, ch 158, sc in 2nd ch from hook, sc in each ch across, turn (157).

Note: For **shell** *(see fig. 22, page 157),* (2 dc, ch 1, 2 dc) in next st.

Row 2: Ch 3, *skip next 2 sts, shell, skip next 2 sts, dc in next st; repeat from * across, turn (27 dc, 26 shells).

Row 3: Ch 3, shell in ch sp of each shell and dc in each dc across with dc in top of ch-3, turn.

Row 4: Ch 5, sc in next shell, ch 2, dc in next dc, *ch 2, sc in next shell, ch 2, dc in next dc; repeat from * across, turn.

Row 5: Ch 3, dc in each sc, dc in each dc and 2 dc in each ch sp across, turn (157).

Row 6: Ch 1, sc in first st, skip next 2 sts, sc in next st, (ch 2, skip next 2 sts, sc in next st) across (53 sc, 52 ch sps).

Row 7: Ch 3, 2 dc in each ch sp and dc in each sc across, turn (157).

Rows 8-58: Repeat rows 2-7 consecutively, ending with row 4.

Row 59: Ch 1, sc in each dc, sc in each sc and 2 sc in each ch sp across, **do not** turn, fasten off (157).

Row 60: For **first side,** join dk. teal with sc in first st, sc in each st across, **do not** turn, fasten off.

Rows 61-62: Working in color sequence of rose and dk. teal, repeat row 60. For **second side,** working on opposite side of row 1, repeat rows 60-62 of first side.

Rosebud Trim

Row 1: Working across row 6, around post of each sc, join rose with sl st around first st, ch 3, *sl st around next st, ch 1; for **rosebud,** 5 sc around same st, drop lp from hook, insert hook in first st of 5-sc group, draw dropped lp through st; ch 3; repeat from * across to last sc, sl st around last sc, fasten off.

Rnd 2: Working around rosebuds, join dk. teal with sl st around first sc on row 6 of afghan, (ch 3, sl st around next sc) across, ch 1; working on opposite side of rosebuds, sc around same st, (ch 3, sl st around next st) across, ch 1, join with sl st in first sl st, fasten off. Pull each rosebud up through sps on rnd 2.

Repeat Rosebud Trim across rows 12, 18, 24, 30, 36, 42, 48 and 54.

continued on page 117

Shades of Green

by designer Dorris Brooks

This pretty afghan, with its reserved traditional styling of vertical stripes in teal tones, is quick and easy enough to finish in a weekend.

Finished Size

51" x 67" without fringe.

Materials

Worsted-weight yarn — 17 oz. each dk. green and med. green, 13 oz. lt. green; tapestry needle; I crochet hook or size needed to obtain gauge.

Gauge

3 dc sts = 1"; 3 dc rows = 2".

Skill Level

★ Easy

Instructions

Afghan

Notes: Ch-3 at beginning of each row counts as first stitch.

For **V-stitch (V-st)** *(see fig. 25, page 158),* (dc, ch 1, dc) in next st.

Row 1: With med. green, ch 203, dc in 4th ch from hook, dc in each ch across, turn (201).

Row 2: Ch 3, (skip next st, V-st, skip next st, dc in next st) across, turn (51 dc, 50 V-sts).

Row 3: Ch 3, dc in same st, dc in ch-1 sp of next V-st, (V-st in next dc between V-sts, dc in ch-1 sp of next V-st) across with 2 dc in last st, turn (54 dc, 49 V-sts).

Row 4: Ch 3, dc in each dc and in each ch-1 sp across, turn, fasten off (201).

Row 5: Join lt. green with sl st in first st, ch 4, skip next st, dc in next st, (ch 1, skip next st, dc in next st) across, turn (101 dc, 100 ch-1 sps).

Row 6: Ch 4, (dc in next dc, ch 1) across with dc in 3rd ch of last ch-4, turn, fasten off.

Row 7: Join dk. green with sl st in first st, ch 3, dc in each ch-1 sp and in each st across, turn (201).

Rows 8-12: Repeat rows 2-6.

Row 13: With med. green, repeat row 7.

Rows 14-76: Repeat rows 2-13, ending with row 4. Fasten off at end of last row.

Fringe

For **each fringe,** cut four strands yarn each 16" long. With all four strands held together, fold in half, insert hook over stitch at end of row, draw fold through, draw all loose ends through fold, tighten. Trim ends.

Fringe in end of each row on short ends of afghan, matching colors.∞

Rosebuds in Rows continued from page 115

Fringe (make 22)

For **each fringe,** cut ten strands rose each 15" long. With all ten strands held together, fold in half, insert hook in st, draw fold through, draw all loose ends through fold, tighten. Trim ends.

Fringe in ends of row 62 on first and second side of afghan in end of rosebud rows on both sides of afghan.∞

Wine & Roses

by designer Daisy Watson

Drape this classic, shell-stitch afghan across a sofa or bed for a distinctive accent. Pick up coordinating colors from upholstery fabrics or wallpaper for a decorator touch.

Finished Size

44" x 66" not including fringe.

Materials

Worsted-weight yarn — 32½ oz. rose and 29 oz. wine; tapestry needle; I crochet hook or size needed to obtain gauge.

Gauge

7 shells and sc = 10"; 7 pattern rows = 4".

Skill Level

★★ Average

Instructions

Afghan

Notes: For **shell,** 5 dc in next st.

For **inverted shell (inv shell),** (yo, insert hook in next st, yo, draw lp through, yo, draw through 2 lps on hook) 5 times, yo, draw through all 6 lps on hook.

Row 1: With wine, ch 184, 2 dc in 4th ch from hook, skip next 2 chs, sc in next ch, skip next 2 chs, (shell in next ch, skip next 2 chs, sc in next ch, skip next 2 chs) across with 3 dc in last ch, **do not** turn, fasten off (30 sc, 29 shells, 2 half shells).

Row 2: Join rose with sc in first st, (ch 2, inv shell, ch 2, sc in next st) across, turn, fasten off (31 sc, 30 inv shells).

Row 3: Join wine with sl st in first st, ch 3, 2 dc in same st, skip next ch sp, sc in next inv shell, skip next ch sp, (shell in next sc, skip next ch sp, sc in next inv shell, skip next ch sp) across with 3 dc in last st, **do not** turn, fasten off (30 sc, 29 shells, 2 half shells).

Rows 4-115: Repeat rows 2 and 3 alternately.

For **edging,** working in end of rows, join rose with sl st in row 1, shell in next row, (skip next row, 3 sc in next row, skip next row, shell in next row) across with sl st in last row, fasten off. Repeat on other side.

Fringe

For **each fringe,** cut four strands each wine and rose each 10" long. With all eight strands held together, fold in half, insert hook in st, draw fold through, draw all loose ends through fold, tighten. Trim ends.

Fringe in each sc and in first and last sts on each short end of afghan.

Marvelous Motifs

*From Granny squares to stylized floral
motifs and beyond, these beautiful block
designs are perfect take-along projects.
Create a lacy, delicate afghan reminiscent
of Grandmother's flower garden, or choose
a glorious Victorian masterpiece made of
hexagonal "posy" motifs.*

Posy Perfect

by designer Diane Simpson

Easy hexagonal blocks in tan, pale green, purple and yellow are as fresh as a field full of wildflowers in bloom. Extra-long fringe makes the afghan drape beautifully.

Finished Size

Each Hexagon is 7" across. Afghan is 56" x 68" not including fringe.

Materials

Worsted-weight yarn — 32 oz. peach, 18 oz. pale green, 9 oz. purple, 6 oz. yellow; tapestry needle; G crochet hook or size needed to obtain gauge.

Gauge

Rnd 1 = 2½" across.

Skill Level

★ Easy

Instructions

Hexagon (make 83)

Rnd 1: With yellow, ch 5, sl st in first ch to form ring, ch 4, 17 tr in ring, join with sl st in top of ch-4, fasten off (18).

Rnd 2: Join purple with sl st in first st, ch 4, 6 tr in same st, skip next 2 sts, (7 tr in next st, skip next 2 sts) around, join as before, fasten off (42 tr).

Rnd 3: Join pale green with sl st in 4th tr of first 7-tr group, ch 3, 2 dc in same st, *skip next 3 sts, 7 tr in space between next two 7-tr groups, skip next 3 sts*, [3 dc in next st; repeat between **]; repeat between [ ] around, join with sl st in top of ch-3, fas-

ten off (42 tr, 18 dc).

Rnd 4: Join peach with sl st in 4th tr of any 7-tr group, ch 3, 4 dc in same st, dc in next 9 sts, (5 dc in next st, dc in next 9 sts) around, join, fasten off (84 dc).

To **assemble,** sew Hexagons together as shown in Assembly Diagram below.

For **each fringe,** cut three strands peach each 24" long. With all three strands held together, fold in half, insert hook in st, draw fold through, draw all loose ends through fold, tighten. Trim ends.

Fringe in each st and in each seam on short ends of afghan.∞

ASSEMBLY DIAGRAM

Granny's Flowers

by designer Carolyn Brooks Christmas

Get out your scrap bag and choose bright floral shades for this stunning Granny Square variation. Brown centers and a beige background create homespun charm.

Finished Size

48" x 72" without fringe.

Materials

Worsted-weight yarn — 27 oz. beige, 7 oz. dk. brown, 2 oz. each of 12 different lt. and dk. color combinations *(see note below)*; tapestry needle; K crochet hook or size needed to obtain gauge.

Gauge

One motif measures 6" square.

Skill Level

★ Easy

Instructions

Motif (make 8 squares each of lt. and dk. color combinations or 96 squares)

Note: Rnd 2 uses 4½ yds. (more or less) of yarn to complete. Rnd 3 uses 6 yds. (more or less) of yarn to complete.

Rnd 1: With dk. brown, ch 2, 8 sc in 2nd ch from hook, join with sl st in first sc (8).

Rnd 2: Ch 4, dc in same st, (dc, ch 1, dc) in each st around, join with sl st in 3rd ch of ch-4, fasten off (16 dc).

Rnd 3: Join lt. color with sl st in any ch sp, ch 3, (dc, ch 1, 2 dc) in same sp, ch 1, *(2 dc, ch 1, 2 dc) in next ch sp, ch 1; repeat from * around, join with sl st in top of ch-3, fasten off (32 dc, 16 ch sps).

Rnd 4: Join dk. color with sc in first ch sp, 5 dc in next ch sp, *sc in next ch sp, 5 dc in next ch sp; repeat from * around, join with sl st in first sc, fasten off (40 dc, 8 sc).

Rnd 5: Join beige with sc in 3rd dc of any 5-dc group, *hdc in next dc, dc in next dc; for **corner,** (2 tr, ch 2, 2 tr) in next sc; dc in next dc, hdc in next dc, sc in next dc, skip next 2 dc, (dc, hdc, sc, hdc, dc) in next sc, skip next 2 dc*, [sc in next dc; repeat between **]; repeat between [ ] around, join with sl st in first sc, fasten off.

Sew motifs together in 12 rows of eight squares each.

For **each fringe,** cut two strands beige each 16" long. With both strands held together, fold in half, insert hook in st, draw fold through, draw all loose ends through fold, tighten. Trim ends.

Fringe in each st on short ends of afghan. ∞

Summer Flowers

by designer Carolyn Brooks Christmas

Welcome the new baby with this cloud-soft afghan. Reminiscent of European tiles, these stylized Granny Squares are edged with delicate shells.

Finished Size

Each square is 4¾". Afghan is 34" x 37".

Materials

3-ply baby yarn — 8 oz. white, 6 oz. each peach and blue, 2 oz. yellow; tapestry needle; G crochet hook or size needed to obtain gauge.

Gauge

4 dc = 1"; 2 dc rnds = 1".

Skill Level

★ Easy

Instructions

Square (make 56)

Note: The afghan pictured is made with 56 squares; however, you may make as many as desired.

Rnd 1: With yellow, ch 4, sl st in first ch to form ring, ch 4, (dc in ring, ch 1) 7 times, join with sl st in 3rd ch of ch-4, fasten off (8).

Rnd 2: Join white with sl st in any ch-1 sp, ch 3, 2 dc in same sp, ch 1, (3 dc in next ch-1 sp, ch 1) around, join, fasten off (24 dc).

Rnd 3: Join peach with sl st in any ch-1 sp, ch 3, 4 dc in same sp, skip next st, sc in next st, (5 dc in next ch-1 sp, skip next st, sc in next st) around, join, fasten off (40 dc, 8 sc).

Rnd 4: Join blue with sl st in any sc, ch 3, 4 dc in same st, skip next 2 dc, sc in next dc, skip next 2 dc, (5 dc in next sc, skip next 2 dc, sc in next dc, skip next 2 dc) around, join, fasten off.

Rnd 5: Join white with sl st in any sc, ch 5, (tr, ch 1) 4 times in same st, skip next 2 sts, sc in next 7 sts, skip next 2 sts, *(tr, ch 1) 5 times in next st, skip next 2 sts, sc in next 7 sts, skip next 2 sts; repeat from * around, join, fasten off (20 tr, 28 sc).

Holding wrong sides together, working through both thicknesses, matching sts, sew squares together in eight rows of seven squares each.

For **trim,** join peach with sc in any st, skip next st or next ch-1 sp, 5 dc in next st, skip next st or next ch-1 sp, (sc in next st, skip next st or ch-1 sp, 5 dc in next st, skip next st or next ch-1 sp) around, join, fasten off (124 5-dc groups). ❧

Lush & Lovely

by designer Shep Shepherd

Like an old-fashioned quilt, this afghan is soft and cozy and will brighten up your favorite room. A generously ruffled border graces all sides with country elegance.

Finished Size

50" x 58".

Materials

Fuzzy worsted-weight yarn — 21½ oz. peach; 11 oz. apricot and 7 oz. dk. blue; tapestry needle; J crochet hook or size needed to obtain gauge.

Gauge

5 dc sts = 2"; 3 dc rnds = 2".

Skill Level

★★ Average

Instructions

Block (make 12)

Row 1: With peach, ch 10, hdc in 3rd ch from hook, hdc in each ch across, turn (9 hdc).

Rows 2-5: Ch 2, hdc in each st across, turn. **Do not** turn or fasten off at end of last row.

Rnd 6: Working around outer edge, ch 1, (skip ends of next 2 rows, 9 tr in end of next row, skip ends of next 2 rows, sc in next st, skip next 3 sts, 9 tr in next st, skip next 3 sts, sc in next st) 2 times, join with sl st in first tr, fasten off (36 tr, 4 sc).

Rnd 7: Join dk. blue with sl st in any sc, ch 2, 2 hdc in same st, *ch 2, skip next 2 tr, sc in next tr, ch 2, skip next st, (2 hdc, ch 2, 2 hdc) in next tr, ch 2, skip next tr, sc in next tr, ch 2, skip next 2 tr*, [3 hdc in next sc; repeat between **]; repeat between [ ] around, join with sl st in top of ch-2, fasten off (28 hdc, 8 sc).

Rnd 8: Join apricot with sl st in last sc made, ch 4, 6 tr in same st, *skip next ch-2 sp, skip next st, sc in next st, skip next st, skip next ch-2 sp, 7 tr in next sc, skip next ch-2 sp, sc in next ch-2 sp, skip next ch-2 sp*, [7 tr in next sc; repeat between **]; repeat between [ ] around, join with sl st in top of ch-4 (56 tr, 8 sc).

Rnd 9: Join peach with sc in 4th tr of last 7-tr group made, *(ch 1, skip next st, sc in next st) 4 times, ch 1, skip next 3 sts, (3 tr, ch 2, 3 tr) in next st, ch 1, skip next 3 sts*, [sc in next st; repeat between **]; repeat between [ ] around, join with sl st in first sc (20 sc, 24 tr).

Rnd 10: Ch 2, hdc in each st and in each ch-1 sp around with (2 hdc, ch 2, 2 hdc) in each ch-2 sp, join, fasten off (84).

Assembly

With wrong sides together, working through both thicknesses and in **back lps** *(see fig. 1, page 154)*, sc Blocks together in four rows of three Blocks each.

Edging

Rnd 1: Working around outer edge, join dk. blue with sc in any st, sc in each st and in each seam around with (sc, ch 2, sc) in each corner, join with sl st in first sc, fasten off.

Rnd 2: Join apricot with sl st in any st, ch 2, hdc in each st around with (2 hdc, ch 2, 2 hdc)

continued on page 135

Jeweled Motifs

by designer Fran Rohus

This contemporary throw almost sparkles with the glowing colors of amethyst, jade, sapphire and ruby. An onyx background displays each block like precious stones.

Finished Size

Each motif is 6" across. Afghan is 40" x 52".

Materials

Worsted-weight yarn — 20 oz. black, 8 oz. each pink, purple, blue and green; tapestry needle; G crochet hook or size needed to obtain gauge.

Gauge

4 dc sts = 1"; 2 dc rows = 1".

Skill Level

★ Easy

Instructions

Motif A (make 12)

Rnd 1: With purple, ch 6, sl st in first ch to form ring, ch 4, tr in ring, ch 1, (2 tr in ring, ch 1) 7 times, join with sl st in top of ch-4, fasten off (16 tr, 8 ch sps).

Rnd 2: Join pink with sl st in any ch sp, (ch 3, dc, ch 2, 2 dc) in same sp, ch 2, skip next 2 sts, sc in next ch sp, ch 2, skip next 2 sts, *(2 dc, ch 2, 2 dc) in next ch sp, ch 2, sc in next ch sp, ch 2; repeat from * around, join with sl st in top of ch-3, fasten off (16 dc, 4 sc, 12 ch sps).

Note: For **single crochet front post (sc fp)** *(see fig. 23, page 158)*, insert hook from front to back around post of st on previous row, complete as sc.

Rnd 3: Join black with sl st in first ch sp, (ch 3, 2 dc, ch 1, 3 dc) in same sp, ch 3, sc fp around next sc, ch 3, skip next ch sp, *(3 dc, ch 1, 3 dc) in next ch sp, ch 3, sc fp around next sc, ch 3, skip next ch sp; repeat from * around, join, fasten off (24 dc, 4 sc fp, 12 ch sps).

Rnd 4: Join green with sl st in first st, ch 3, dc in each of next 2 sts, (ch 3, sc in next ch-1 sp, ch 3, dc in each of next 3 sts, ch 3, sc in next ch-3 sp, ch 3, sc fp around next sc, ch 3, sc in next ch sp, ch 3), *dc in each of next 3 sts; repeat between ( ); repeat from * around, join, fasten off (24 dc, 12 sc, 4 sc fp, 24 ch sps).

Rnd 5: Join blue with sl st in first st, ch 3, dc in each of next 2 sts, *ch 3, sc fp around next st, ch 3, dc in each of next 3 sts, ch 3, (sc fp around next st, ch 3) 3 times*, [dc in each of next 3 sts; repeat between **]; repeat between [ ] around, join, fasten off (24 dc, 16 sc fp, 24 ch sps).

Rnd 6: With black, repeat rnd 5, **do not** fasten off.

Rnd 7: Sl st to first ch sp, (ch 3, 2 dc) in same sp, *ch 4, skip next sc, 3 dc in next ch sp, ch 4, skip next 3 dc, 2 dc in each of next 4 ch sps, ch 4, skip next 3 dc*, [3 dc in next ch sp; repeat between **]; repeat between [ ] around, join, fasten off.

Motif B (make 12)

Rnds 1-5: Working in color sequence of blue, purple, black, pink and green, repeat same rnds of Motif A.

Rnds 6-7: Repeat same rnds of Motif A.

continued on page 135

Texas Star

by designer Sandra Smith

With its bright scheme and quilt-like design, this afghan is sure to be a star attraction in your home. The pleasing zigzag edge adds interest and appeal.

Finished Size

81" x 84".

Materials

Worsted-weight yarn — 80 oz. black, 10 oz. red, 6 oz. yellow, 4 oz. each lt. blue, dk. blue, lt. purple, dk. purple, lt. green and dk. green; tapestry needle; F crochet hook or size needed to obtain gauge.

Gauge

9 sc sts = 2"; 9 sc rows = 2".

Skill Level

★★ Average

Instructions

Diamond (make 1,106, see list below)

Note: Make diamonds in the following amounts and colors:

520 Black	60 Dk. Green	60 Lt. Blue
148 Red	60 Lt. Green	60 Dk. Purple
78 Yellow	60 Dk. Blue	60 Lt. Purple

Row 1: Ch 9, sc in 2nd ch from hook, sc in each ch across, turn (8).

Row 2: Ch 1, skip first st, sc in next 6 sts, 2 sc in last st, turn (8).

Row 3: Ch 1, 2 sc in first st, sc in next 5 sts, sc last 2 sts tog, turn (8).

Rows 4-5: Repeat rows 2 and 3. Fasten off at end of last row.

Joining Rnd

For **first border,** join black with sc in any st of yellow diamond, sc in each st and in end of each row around with (sc, ch 2, sc) in each corner st, join with sl st in first sc, fasten off (32 sc).

Note: For **joining ch-2 sp,** ch 1, sl st in next ch-2 sp on previous diamond, ch 1.

For **next border,** work same as first border joining diamonds together according to Diagram No. 1 shown below. Continue working in color pattern according to Diagram No. 2 shown below, joining diamonds together.

Edging

Rnd 1: Working around entire outer edge, join black with sc in any corner ch sp, (ch 1, sc) in same sp, sc in each st around with (sc, ch 1 sc) in each corner ch sp and sc next 2 sts tog at each joining, join with sl st in first sc, fasten off.

Rnd 2: With yellow, repeat rnd 1.

Rnd 3: With red, repeat rnd 1.∾

ASSEMBLY DIAGRAM

DIAGRAM NO.1

DIAGRAM NO. 2

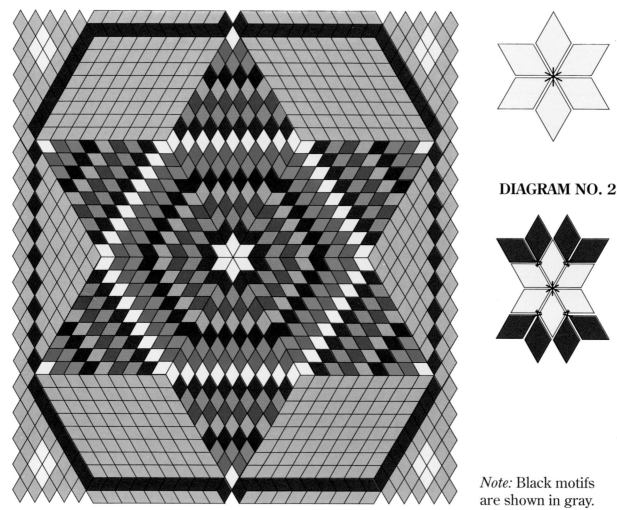

Note: Black motifs are shown in gray.

Lush & Lovely continued from page 129

in each ch-2 sp, join with sl st in top of ch-2, fasten off.

Rnd 3: Join dk. blue with sc in any st, sc in each st around with (sc, ch 2, sc) in each ch-2 sp, join with sc in first sc, fasten off.

Rnd 4: Join peach with sl st in any st, ch 3, dc in each st around with (2 dc, ch 2, 2 dc) in each ch-2 sp, join with sl st in top of ch-3.

Rnds 5-12: Ch 3, dc in each st around with (2 dc, ch 2, 2 dc) in each ch-2 sp, join. Fasten off at end of last rnd.

Rnds 13-15: Repeat rnds 3 and 2 alternately, ending with rnd 3.

Note: For **double treble crochet (dtr)** *(see fig. 8, page 155),* yo 3 times, insert hook in st, yo, draw lp through, (yo, draw through 2 lps on hook) 4 times.

Rnd 16: Join apricot with sl st in any st, ch 6, dtr in same st, ch 1, (dtr, ch 1, dtr, ch 1) in each st and in each ch-2 sp around, join with sl st in 5th ch of ch-6.

Rnd 17: Ch 6, (dtr in next st, ch 1) around, join, fasten off.∽

Jeweled Motifs continued from page 131

Motif C (make 12)
Rnds 1-5: Working in color sequence of pink, green, black, blue and purple, repeat same rnds of Motif A.

Rnds 6-7: Repeat same rnds of Motif A.

Motif D (make 12)
Rnds 1-5: Working in color sequence of green, blue, black, purple and pink, repeat same rnds of Motif A.

Rnds 6-7: Repeat same rnds of Motif A.

Matching sts and chs, sew motifs together according to diagram at right.

Edging
Rnd 1: Join black with sl st in top right corner ch sp, ch 3, (2 dc, ch 2, 3 dc) in same sp, [*◊dc in each of next 3 sts, 3 dc in next ch sp, dc in next 8 sts, 3 dc in next ch sp, dc in each of next 3 sts◊, 2 dc in each of next 2 ch sps*; repeat between ** 4 times; repeat between ◊ ◊ one time, (3 dc, ch 2, 3 dc) in next ch sp; repeat between ** 7 times; repeat between ◊ ◊ one more time], (3 dc, ch 2, 3 dc) in next ch sp; repeat between [ ] one time, join with sl st in top of ch-3 (680 dc).

Rnds 2-3: Ch 3, dc in each st around with (3 dc, ch 2, 3 dc) in each corner ch sp, join, ending with 728 dc.

Note: For **picot,** *(see fig. 21, page 157),* ch 3, sc in 2nd ch from hook, ch 1.

Rnd 4: Ch 1, sc in first st, picot, sc in next 5 sts, picot, *sc in each of next 3 sts, (sc, picot, sc) in next ch sp, sc in next 4 sts, picot, (sc in next 5 sts, picot) 30 times, sc in next 4 sts, (sc, picot, sc) in next ch sp, sc in each of next 3 sts, picot*, (sc in next 5 sts, picot) 40 times; repeat between **, (sc in next 5 sts, picot) 38 times, sc in last 4 sts, join, fasten off.∽

ASSEMBLY DIAGRAM

D	A	B	C	D	A
C	D	A	B	C	D
B	C	D	A	B	C
A	B	C	D	A	B
D	A	B	C	D	A
C	D	A	B	C	D
B	C	D	A	B	C
A	B	C	D	A	B

Cozy Quilts

Nothing adds country charm to a room
like an old-fashioned quilt. Whether it
features the charm of patchwork
or the fascination of a carefully planned
design, a quilt afghan is a welcome
companion on a quiet afternoon spent
reading or napping.

Triangle Treasure

by designer Rosalie DeVries

Reminiscent of the classic "Goose Tracks" quilt pattern, this striking creation will be the focal point of any room. The vertical pattern is continued with the plush fringe.

Finished Size

45" x 63" without fringe.

Materials

Worsted-weight yarn — 22 oz. each lt. green and tan, 9 oz. each dk. green and white; tapestry needle; F crochet hook or size needed to obtain gauge.

Gauge

One tr = 1¼" tall; Rows 1 and 2 = 1¼" wide.

Skill Level

★★ Average

Instructions

Afghan

Row 1: With dk. green, ch 5, 4 tr in 5th ch from hook, (ch 6, 4 tr in 5th ch from hook) 41 times, ch 1, **do not** turn, fasten off (42 tr groups, 42 ch-1 sps).

Note: For **double treble crochet (dtr),** *(see fig. 8, page 155),* yo 3 times, insert hook in st, yo, draw lp through, (yo, draw through 2 lps on hook) 4 times.

Row 2: Join lt. green with sl st in top of starting ch-5 on first tr group made on last row, *sc in next tr, hdc in next tr, dc in next tr, tr in next tr, dtr in next ch-1 sp*, [sl st in top of next ch-5; repeat between **]; repeat between [ ] across, **turn** (252 sts).

Row 3: Ch 5, 4 tr in 5th ch from hook, skip first 4 sts, sl st in next sc, *ch 1, skip next sl st, sl st in next dtr, ch 5, 4 tr in 5th ch from hook, skip next 3 sts, sl st in next sc; repeat from * across with sl st in last sl st, **do not** turn, fasten off.

Row 4: Join tan with sl st in top of starting ch-5 on first tr group made on last row, *sc in next tr, hdc in next tr, dc in next tr, tr in next tr*, [dtr in next ch-1 sp, sl st in top of next ch-5; repeat between **]; repeat between [ ] across to last 2 sl sts, skip next sl st, dtr in last sl st, **turn.**

Rows 5-72: Working in color sequence of white, tan, lt. green, dk. green, lt. green and tan, repeat rows 3 and 4 alternately. At end of last row, **do not** turn.

Row 73: For **first side,** ch 1, reverse sc in each st across, fasten off. For **second side,** working on opposite side of row 1, join with sc in first st, reverse sc in each ch and 4 reverse sc over each tr across, fasten off.

Fringe

For **each fringe,** cut two strands same-color yarn each 8" long. With both strands held together, fold in half, insert hook in sp, draw fold through sp, draw all loose ends through fold, tighten. Trim ends.

Matching colors, make one fringe in end of each sl st row and 2 fringe over each ch-5 sp or dtr on short sides of afghan. ∞

Quilter's Star

by designer Kathleen Bernier Williford

Capture the patriotic spirit in this bold and bright throw. It's gorgeous made with either 100% cotton or acrylic yarn, and is just right for summer decorating.

Finished Size

46½" x 53¼".

Materials

100% cotton worsted-weight yarn — 35 oz. white, 18 oz. red, 7 oz. blue; one 14" square pillow form; tapestry needle; H crochet hook or size needed to obtain gauge.

Gauge

7 sc sts = 2"; 7 sc rows = 2".

Skill Level

★★ Average

Instructions

Block (make 4)

Row 1: With white, ch 53, sc in 2nd ch from hook, sc in each ch across, turn (52).

Note: When changing colors *(see fig. 13, page 156),* always drop all colors to same side of work. **Do not** carry dropped colors across to next section of same color. Use a separate ball of yarn for each color section.

Rows 2-52: Ch 1, sc in each st across changing colors according to Star Graph above, turn.

Rnd 53: Working around outer edge, ch 1, sc in end of each row and in each st around with 3 sc in each corner, join with sl st in first sc, **do not**

STAR GRAPH

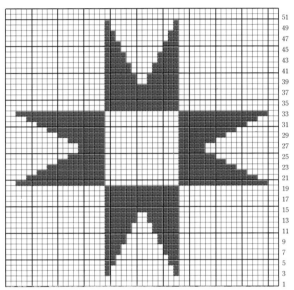

51
49
47
45
43
41
39
37
35
33
31
29
27
25
23
21
19
17
15
13
11
9
7
5
3
1

turn, fasten off.

Rnd 54: Join red with sl st in any st, ch 3, dc in each st around with 5 dc in each corner, join with sl st in top of ch-3.

Rnds 55-56: Ch 3, dc in each st around with 5 dc in each corner, join. Fasten off at end of last rnd.

Strip (make 3)

Row 1: With red, ch 131, dc in 4th ch from hook, dc in each ch across, turn (129).

Rows 2-3: Ch 3, dc in each st across, turn. Fasten off at end of last row.

Sew Blocks and Srips together as shown in Assembly Diagram on page 149.

Edging

Rnd 1: Working around outer edge of afghan,

continued on page 149

Pretty Pinwheel

by designer Katherine Eng

If you love the purely American look of patchwork quilts, you'll adore this interpretation of patchwork in crochet. Choose pleasing color combinations of knitting worsted yarn.

Finished Size

51" x 66".

Materials

Worsted-weight yarn — 25 oz. each lt. teal and lavender, 4 oz. each slate blue, dk. red and lt. red, small amounts of 22 different pinwheel colors in blues, greens, pinks, plums and reds; tapestry needle; G crochet hook or size needed to obtain gauge.

Gauge

4 sc sts = 1"; 4 sc rows = 1".

Skill Level

★★★ Challenging

Instructions

Block (make 12)
Pinwheels

Notes: Use some red in each pinwheel to balance pattern with border.

Pinwheels may cup slightly until corners are added.

Row 1: For **first wedge,** with first color, ch 16, sc in 2nd ch from hook, sc in each ch across, turn (15).

Row 2: Ch 1, sc in each st across to last 2 sts, sc last 2 sts tog, turn (14).

Row 3: Ch 1, sc first 2 sts tog, sc in each st across, turn (13).

Rows 4-14: Repeat rows 2 and 3 alternately, ending with row 2 and 2 sts.

Row 15: Ch 1, sc first 2 sts tog, fasten off (1).

Row 1: For **second wedge,** with right side facing you, working in ends of rows, join next color with sc in row 6 on slanted edge of last wedge made, 2 sc in next row, (sc in next row, 2 sc in next row) across, turn (15).

Row 2: Ch 1, sc first 2 sts tog, sc in each st across, turn (14).

Row 3: Ch 1, sc in each st across to last 2 sts, sc last 2 sts tog, turn (13).

Rows 4-14: Repeat rows 2 and 3 alternately, ending with row 2 and 2 sts.

Row 15: Ch 1, sc first 2 sts tog, fasten off (1).

Row 1: For **third wedge,** with right side facing you, working in ends of rows, join next color with sc in row 10 on slanted edge of last wedge made, 2 sc in next row, (sc in next row, 2 sc in next row) across, turn (15).

Rows 2-15: Repeat same rows of second wedge.

For **fourth, fifth, sixth** and **seventh wedges,** work same as Third Wedge.

Row 1: For **eighth wedge,** with right side facing you, working in ends of rows, join with sc in row 10 on slanted edge of last wedge made, 2 sc in next row, (sc in next row, 2 sc in next row) across, sl st in rows 15 and 14 of First Wedge, turn (15 sc, 2 sl sts).

Row 2: Ch 1, skip first 2 sl sts, sc first 2 sc tog, sc in each sc across, turn.

Row 3: Ch 1, sc in each sc across to last 2 sts, sc last 2 sc tog, skip next 2 rows of First Wedge,

Heart & Home

by designer Kathleen Bernier Williford

Down-home country style is yours with this pretty afghan. Alternate blocks feature big, appliqué-type hearts, while remaining blocks display the popular house motif.

Finished Size

57½" x 76".

Materials

Fuzzy worsted-weight yarn — 39 oz. off-white, 16 oz. each lt. green, dk. green and pink; tapestry needle; J crochet hook or size needed to obtain gauge.

Gauge

5 sc sts = 2"; 5 sc rows = 2".

Skill Level

★★ Average

Instructions

Home Square (make 6)

Notes: Make Home Squares in color combinations as shown in Assembly Diagram on page 149.

Wind lt. green into three balls of 20 yds. each. Wind dk. green into three balls of 20 yds. each. Wind off-white into three balls of 20 yds. each.

When changing colors *(see fig. 13, page 156),* always drop all colors to same side of work. **Do not** carry dropped colors across to next section of same color. Use a separate ball of yarn for each color section. Fasten off at end of each color section.

Row 1: With first color, ch 43, sc in 2nd ch

from hook, sc in each ch across, turn (42).

Rows 2-42: Ch 1, sc in each st across changing colors according to Home Graph below, turn.

Rnd 43: Working around outer edge, ch 1, sc in each st and in end of each row around with 3 sc in each corner, join with sl st in first sc, fasten off.

Rnd 44: Join pink with sc in any st, sc in each st around with 3 sc in center st of each corner, join, fasten off.

Heart Square (make 6)

Note: Make Heart Squares in color combinations as shown in Assembly Diagram on page 149.

Rows 1-42: Repeat same rows of Home Square changing colors according to Heart Graph below, turn.

HOME GRAPH

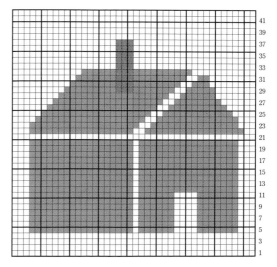

Rnds 43-44: Repeat same rnds of Home Square.

Using tapestry needle and pink, sew Squares together according to Assembly Diagram.

Border

Rnd 1: With wrong side of afghan facing you, working around entire outer edge, join pink with sc in any st, sc in each st around with 3 sc in each corner, join with sl st in first sc, **turn.**

Rnd 2: Ch 3, dc in same st, 2 dc in each st around with 5 dc in each corner, join with sl st in top of ch-3, fasten off.

HEART GRAPH

41
39
37
35
33
31
29
27
25
23
21
19
17
15
13
11
9
7
5
3
1

ASSEMBLY DIAGRAM

Quilter's Star continued from page 141

join white with sl st in any st, ch 3, dc in each st around with 5 dc in each corner, join with sl st in top of ch-3.

Rnd 2: Ch 3, dc in each st around with 5 dc in each corner, join, fasten off.

Rnd 3: Join blue with sl st in any st, ch 3, dc in each st around with 5 dc in each corner, join, fasten off.

Rnd 4: Join white with sl st in any st, ch 3, dc in same st, 2 dc in each st around with 5 dc in each corner, join.

Rnd 5: Repeat rnd 2. ∞

ASSEMBLY DIAGRAM

General Instructions

*Before beginning your afghan,
look over these basic instructions
and stitch illustrations. Whether
you're a novice or an expert,
you'll find everything you need
to know about pattern symbols,
abbreviations and more.*

Yarn

Yarn for afghans is usually baby weight, sport weight, worsted weight or bulky. By using the weight of yarn specified in the pattern, you will be assured of achieving proper gauge. When shopping for yarn, check the label for weight specification. Baby weight and sport weight yarn is usually two or three-ply, while worsted weight is four-ply. Bulky yarns vary in number of plies.

Hooks

Crochet hooks are sized for different weights of yarn, and are available in plastic, wood, aluminum and steel. Most afghans are made with medium and large hooks in plastic, aluminum or wood. Medium-sized hooks are made of plastic or aluminum and are sized from C, the smallest, to K, the largest. Larger hooks are made of plastic, aluminum or wood, and are sized up to size S.

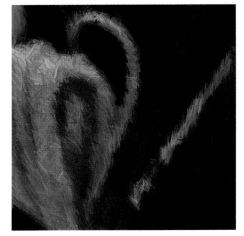

Afghan hooks are similar to knitting needles, except they have a hook on one end. They are sized the same as the hooks mentioned above, and come in various lengths.

The hook size suggested in the pattern is to be used as a guide for determining the hook size you will need. Always work a swatch of an afghan's pattern with the suggested hook size, and if you find the gauge is smaller or larger than that specified in the pattern, choose a different hook size.

Gauge

Always check your gauge before beginning an afghan. The purpose for checking gauge is to determine which hook size to use. The tightness or looseness of your stitches determines gauge, and is affected by hook size. Gauge is measured by counting the number of rows or stitches per inch.

Make a swatch about 4" square in the stitch indicated in the gauge section of the pattern. Lay the swatch flat and measure stitches. If you determine you have more stitches or rows per inch than specified in the pattern, your gauge is too tight and you need to choose a larger hook. If you have fewer stitches per inch than needed, a smaller hook is needed.

For some patterns, especially small patterns like flowers or motifs, gauge is given as a size measurement for the entire motif. In this case, make one motif and measure.

Parentheses, Asterisks & More

For clarity, written instructions may include symbols such as parentheses, asterisks, brackets and diamonds. These symbols are used as signposts to set off a portion of instructions which will be worked more than once.

( ) Parentheses enclose instructions which are to be worked the number of times indicated after the parentheses. For example, "(2 dc in next st, skip next st) 5 times" means to follow the instructions within parentheses a total of five times. Parentheses may also be used to enclose a group of stitches which should be worked in one space or stitch. For example, "(2 dc, ch 2, 2 dc) in next st" means to work all the stitches within parentheses in the next stitch.

*Asterisks may be used alone or in pairs, many times in combination with parentheses. If used in pairs, a set of instructions enclosed within asterisks will be followed by instructions for repeating. These repeat instructions may appear later in the pattern or immediately after the last asterisk. For example, "*Dc in next 4 sts, (2 dc, ch 2, 2 dc) in corner sp*, dc in next 4 sts; repeat between ** 2 times" means to work through the instructions for repeating, then repeat only the instructions that are enclosed within the asterisks twice.

If used alone, an asterisk marks the beginning of instructions which are to be repeated. For example, "Ch 3, dc in same st, *ch 2, skip next 2 sts, dc in next st, ch 1, skip next st, 2 dc in next st; repeat from * across" means to work from the beginning, then repeat only the instructions after the *, working all the way across the row. Instructions for repeating may also specify a number of times to repeat, and this may be followed by further instructions. For example, instructions might say, "...repeat from * 5 more times; dc in last st." To follow these instructions, work through from the beginning once, then repeat from * five more times for a total of six times. Then, follow remaining instructions, which in this example are "dc in last st."

[ ] Brackets and ◊ diamonds are used to clarify and set off sections of instructions.

In some patterns, all types of symbols are used together. As you can see, there is no need to be intimidated by symbols! These signposts will get you where you're going — to the end of a beautiful finished project.

Standard Stitch Abbreviations	
ch(s)	chain(s)
dc	double crochet
dtr	double treble crochet
hdc	half double crochet
lp(s)	loop(s)
rnd(s)	round(s)
sc	single crochet
sl st	slip stitch
sp(s)	space(s)
st(s)	stitch(es)
tog	together
tr	treble crochet
tr tr	triple treble crochet
yo	yarn over

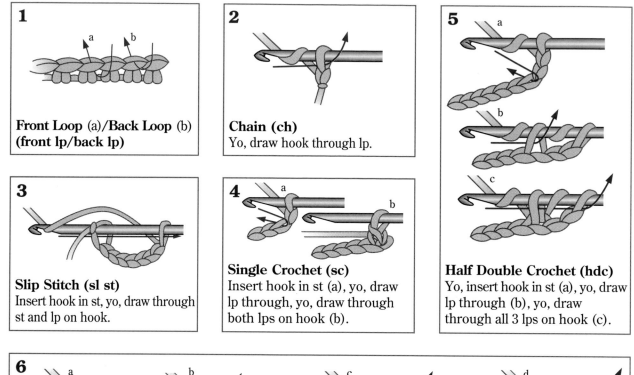

1

Front Loop (a)/**Back Loop** (b)
(front lp/back lp)

2

Chain (ch)
Yo, draw hook through lp.

3

Slip Stitch (sl st)
Insert hook in st, yo, draw through
st and lp on hook.

4

Single Crochet (sc)
Insert hook in st (a), yo, draw
lp through, yo, draw through
both lps on hook (b).

5

Half Double Crochet (hdc)
Yo, insert hook in st (a), yo, draw
lp through (b), yo, draw
through all 3 lps on hook (c).

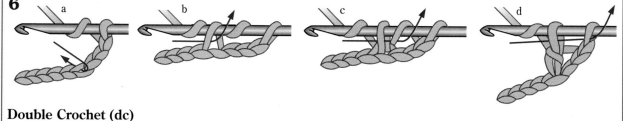

6

Double Crochet (dc)
Yo, insert hook in st (a), yo, draw lp through (b), (yo, draw through 2 lps on hook) 2 times (c and d).

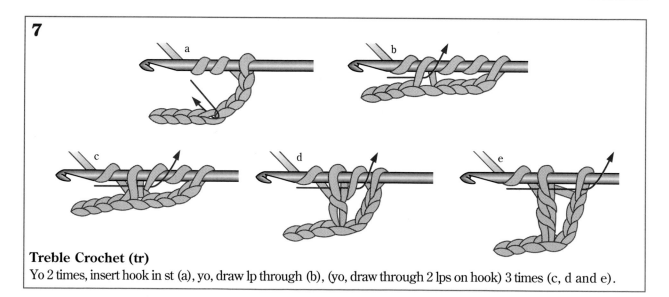

7

Treble Crochet (tr)
Yo 2 times, insert hook in st (a), yo, draw lp through (b), (yo, draw through 2 lps on hook) 3 times (c, d and e).

8

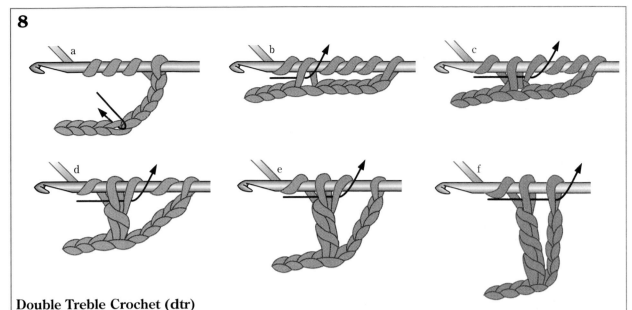

Double Treble Crochet (dtr)
Yo 3 times, insert hook in st (a), yo, draw lp through (b), (yo, draw through 2 lps on hook) 4 times (c, d, e and f).

9

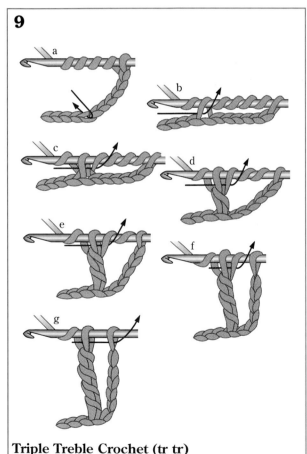

Triple Treble Crochet (tr tr)
Yo 4 times, insert hook in st (a), yo, draw lp through (b), (yo, draw through 2 lps on hook) 5 times (c, d, e, f and g).

10

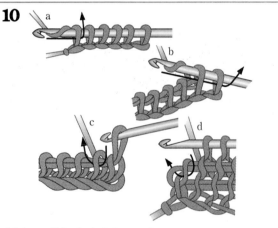

Afghan Stitch (afghan st)
Row 1: Chain number indicated in pattern, insert hook in 2nd ch from hook, yo, draw up ¼" lp, (insert hook in next ch, yo, draw up ¼" lp) across, leaving all lps on hook, **do not** turn; to **work lps off hook**, yo, draw through one lp on hook (a), (yo, draw through 2 lps on hook) across, leaving one lp on hook at end of row (b).

Row 2: Skip first vertical bar; for **afghan stitch,** insert hook under next vertical bar (c), yo, draw up ¼" lp; afghan st in each vertical bar across to last vertical bar; for **last st,** insert hook under last bar and st directly behind it (d), yo, draw up ¼" lp; work lps off hook.

For increase, draw up ¼" lp under first vertical bar.

For decrease, insert hook under next 2 vertical bars, yo, draw through both bars.

11

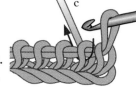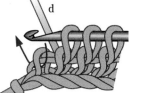

Afghan Knit Stitch (afghan K st)
   Row 1: Work same row of Afghan Stitch.
   Row 2: Skip first vertical bar; for **afghan K st**, insert hook between front and back vertical bars and under horizontal bar of next st (c), draw up a ¼" lp; K across to last vertical bar; for **last st,** insert hook under last bar and st directly behind it (d), yo, draw up ¼" lp; work lps off hook.

CHANGING COLORS

12

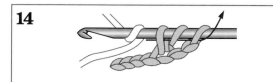

Chain Color Change (ch color change)
Yo with 2nd color, draw through last lp on hook.

13

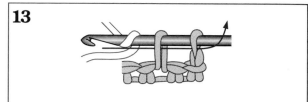

Single Crochet Color Change (sc color change)
Drop first color; yo with 2nd color, draw through last 2 lps of st.

14

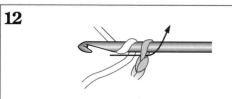

Half Double Crochet Color Change (hdc color change)
Drop first color; yo with 2nd color, draw through last 3 lps of st.

15

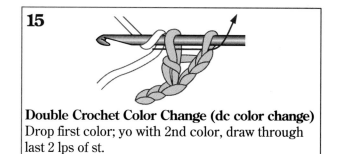

Double Crochet Color Change (dc color change)
Drop first color; yo with 2nd color, draw through last 2 lps of st.

DECREASING

16

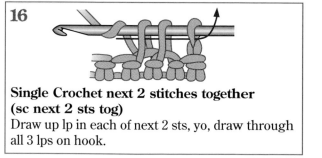

Single Crochet next 2 stitches together (sc next 2 sts tog)
Draw up lp in each of next 2 sts, yo, draw through all 3 lps on hook.

17

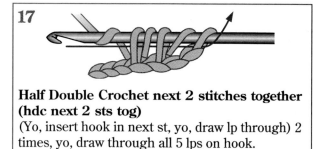

Half Double Crochet next 2 stitches together (hdc next 2 sts tog)
(Yo, insert hook in next st, yo, draw lp through) 2 times, yo, draw through all 5 lps on hook.

18

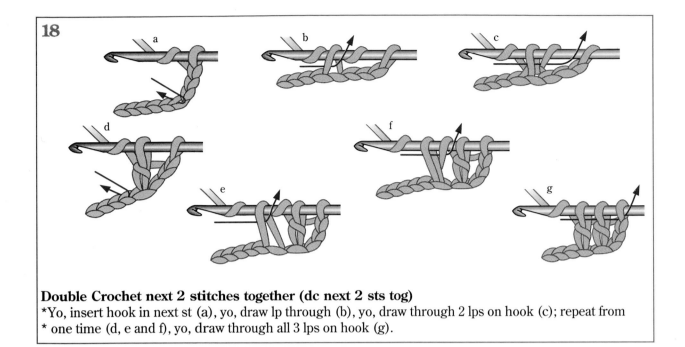

Double Crochet next 2 stitches together (dc next 2 sts tog)
*Yo, insert hook in next st (a), yo, draw lp through (b), yo, draw through 2 lps on hook (c); repeat from
* one time (d, e and f), yo, draw through all 3 lps on hook (g).

SPECIAL STITCHES

19

Cross Stitch (cr st)
Skip next st, dc in next st; working over dc just made, dc in skipped st.

20

Front Cross Stitch (fcr)
Skip next st, dc in next st; working **in front** of dc just made, dc in skipped st.

21

Picot
Ch 3, sl st in 3rd ch from hook.

22

Shell
(2 dc, ch 2, 2 dc) in next st or ch sp.

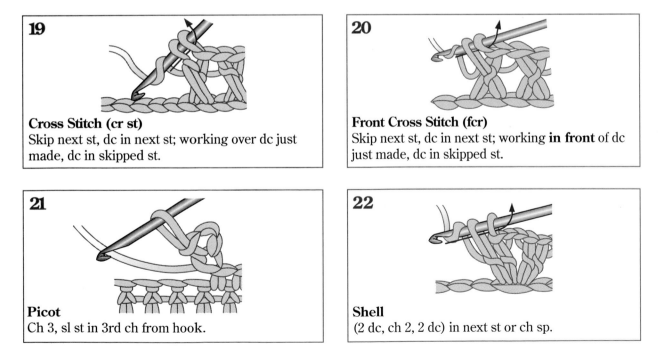

23

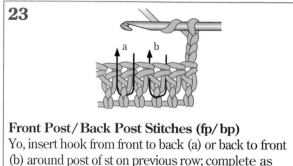

Front Post/Back Post Stitches (fp/bp)
Yo, insert hook from front to back (a) or back to front (b) around post of st on previous row; complete as stated in pattern.

24

Popcorn Stitch (pc)
5 dc in next ch, drop lp from hook, insert hook in first st of 5-dc group, pick up dropped lp, draw through st, ch 1. Push to right side or wrong side of work as needed.

25

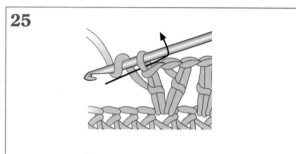

V-Stitch (V-st)
(Dc, ch 1, dc) in next st or ch sp.

26

Puff Stitch (puff st)
Yo, insert hook in next st, yo, draw up ½" long lp, (yo, insert hook in same st, yo, draw up ½" long lp) 2 times, yo, draw through first 7 lps on hook, ch 1.

27

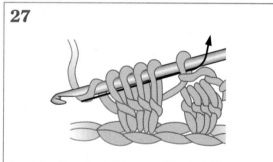

Double Crochet Cluster Stitch (cl)
Yo, insert hook in next st, yo, draw lp through, yo, draw through 2 lps on hook, (yo, insert hook in same st, yo, draw lp through, yo, draw through 2 lps on hook) 3 times, yo, draw through all 5 lps on hook, ch 1.

28

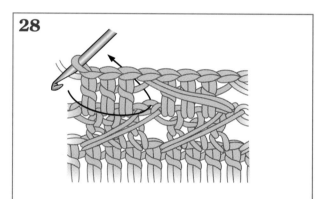

Diagonal Stitch (diagonal st)
Skip next st, dc in each of next 3 sts; working over last 3 sts made, insert hook in skipped st, yo, draw up 1" long lp, yo, draw through both lps on hook.

29

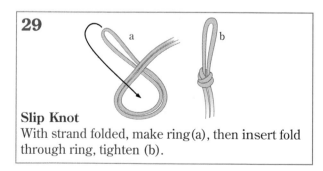

Slip Knot
With strand folded, make ring(a), then insert fold through ring, tighten (b).

30

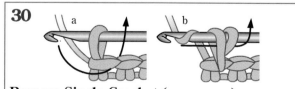

Reverse Single Crochet (reverse sc)
Working from left to right, insert hook in next st to the right (a), yo, draw through st, complete as sc (b).

Joining and Sewing

For joining without sewing, hold pieces wrong sides together and sl st or sc together.

To whipstitch squares or blocks together, hold pieces wrong sides together. Using a #16 or #18 tapestry needle threaded with yarn, beginning in one corner, sew pieces together. Insert needle through inside loops of stitches on first piece, then second piece. For next stitch, go through first piece, then second piece again. Repeat across. Weave in all loose ends.

Blocking

Most afghans do not require professional blocking. To smooth out puckers at seams and give a more finished appearance to the afghan, a light steam pressing works well. Lay afghan on a large table or on the floor and shape and smooth with hands as much as possible. Set iron on permanent press setting and hold iron slightly above stitches, allowing steam to penetrate yarn. Do not rest iron on stitches. Allow to cool and dry completely.

If you prefer professional blocking, choose a cleaning service that specializes in needlework. Request blocking only if you do not want your afghan dry-cleaned. For best results, attach fringe after professional blocking.

Fringe

Cut a piece of cardboard 6" wide and ½" longer than fringe measurement. Wrap yarn evenly around cardboard until filled. Do not wrap too tightly. Cut across one end. Repeat until you have enough fringe for afghan.

For each fringe bundle, hold desired number of strands together and fold in half. To attach fringe, insert hook through wrong side of afghan at edge, draw folded end of strands through, forming loop. Insert loose ends through loop and pull snugly and evenly.

When all fringe is attached, lay afghan on flat surface and trim ends evenly. ∽

Index